VIA Folios 123

READ 'EM AND REAP
Gambling on Italian American Writing

READ 'EM AND REAP
Gambling on Italian American Writing

THE *FRA NOI* REVIEWS 2006-2016

Fred Gardaphé

BORDIGHERA PRESS

Library of Congress Control Number: 2017941323

Cover Photo:
all in, tapis, 2010
by Victor Vic

© 2017 by Fred Gardaphé

All rights reserved. Parts of this book may be reprinted only by written permission from the author, and may not be reproduced for publication in book, magazine, or electronic media of any kind, expect for purposes of literary review by critics.

Printed in the United States.

Published by
BORDIGHERA PRESS
John D. Calandra Italian American Institute
25 West 43rd Street, 17th Floor
New York, NY 10036

VIA FOLIOS 123
ISBN 978-1-59954-119-8

The Gamble of a Literary Life
An Introduction

When I used to play cards, a guy who had a winning hand would throw it down on the table and say, "Read 'em and weep!" I thought of that as I was looking for a title for my third collection of book reviews because for me choosing the literary life has been a lifetime gamble that might not pay off financially, but has always paid off intellectually.

For more than thirty years I have been professionally reviewing books, mostly for the *Fra Noi News*, a remarkable publication. When I first began the *Fra Noi* was edited by Father Armando Pierini (1908 -1998), a tiny, powerhouse of a priest who used the newspaper to connect the Italian American community of Chicago for the purposes of supporting the Villa Scalabrini — a home for the aged that once was exclusively for Italian Americans as they began looking for places outside the home to take care of elderly relatives.

Fr. Pierini was not a trained journalist and thought nothing of clipping articles he liked and pasting them into his publication, never worrying about permissions or legal copyrights. He took whatever he wanted to create pages that were, more often than not, filled with what we called "Grip and Grin" photos of donors handing him checks. Father would sit in the basement of the building where he had his "newsroom" and with the help of Emil Stubitz (1921-2000) produce the monthly paper. He would brew up his "errant" espresso with shots of anisette in his *macchina Faemino* as he doled out assignments in between reflections on his colorful past and correcting my dialect Italian.

But let me take a step back.

In 1978, after my first trip to Italy and being the first in my family to return to my mother's parents' birthplace of Castellana Grotte, I saw my writing take on a new consciousness, a "born again Italian" self awareness, and I was looking for a place to publish it. At my grandmother's suggestion, I called on the priest one day at the Villa. Fr. Pierini knew that grandfather well for he had once found work for the then-unemployed hod carrier, building the Scalabrini Seminary complex, four beautiful brick buildings on spacious green-filled grounds in the Chicago suburb of Stone Park that featured a Calvary Hill Shrine that pilgrims would frequent, climbing the many steps on their knees. Just like my *nonno* got back on his feet with the good Father's help, so I stumbled my way into professional journalism with the same and he put me to work doing the writing he needed. Of course he didn't pay me, and of course he never published my writings; fiction and poetry was not what he was looking for. But once in a while I would convince him to publish a book review I had done mostly because I learned that publishers would send free books if you published reviews; a perfect way for me to feed one of my better habits.

When I wasn't hanging around the Villa, looking for writing to do, I would spend my free time in the library. I often thought about how comfortable I was and fortunate to be doing research in a building that my grandfather had help to construct. What a difference a generation makes! A few years later, Father Lawrence Cozzi (1939-1999) took over for the aging, yet ever-present Pierini.

I had known Larry Cozzi since I was a kid—my buddies and I used to play sports against his team of seminarians. When Cozzi left his job directing the seminary to take over as director of the Villa, he hired James Ylisela, Jr., a budding professional journalist to edit the paper. Jim had an eye for the good story and the right skills to professionalize the *Fra Noi*. When he uncovered a stack of writing I had been sending Fr. Pierini, he invited me to join his newly formed staff. That was back in 1985 and since then, through his editorship, followed by Joe Cosentino, and then Paul M. Basile, the current editor, I have been professionally reviewing books, mostly books written by Italian American writers.

This collection contains most of my Fra Noi reviews written between the years 2006 – 2016. Together with my previous collections, *Dagoes Read: Tradition and the Italian Amerian Writer* (1996) and *The Art of Reading Italian Americana* (2011), it marks the continuation of a lifelong journey that began in 1980 when I found on the E 184 shelf amongst the stacks of Regenstein Library at the University of Chicago Rose Basile Green's *The Italian-American Novel*. In this study it was clear to me that there could be something called Italian American literature, and that it could be professionally studied. That story, recounted in earlier publications, led me away from Walt Whitman and toward Italian American literature as the subject for my eventual dissertation.

Now, as I'm seeing, for the first time, what could be finish line to my career, I want to make sure I have a public record of the deep gratitude I owe to people like Fr. Pierini, Fr. Cozzi, Jim Ylisela, and Joe Cosentino. Paul Basile, the current editor, made the *Fra Noi* the best periodical in Italian Americana. I also would like to thank Mary Racila, *Fra Noi* Creative Director, and the late Florence Bartolomei Roselli, the dedicated volunteer librarian of the Italian Cultural Center, both of whom have helped me in more ways than I can ever say.

Through my life of reading and writing I have reaped many rewards like my good friends and Bordighera co-editors Anthony Julian Tamburri and Paolo Giordano. *Grazie a loro*, and to Nick Grosso, our production editor.

And to you, my lector, may you read these books and reap a rich harvest of thought.

Fred Gardaphe
Bellport, New York

Michael J. Agovino
The Bookmaker (New York: Harper Collins)
ISBN: 978-0-06-1151139-2
October 2009

Don't let the title of Michael J. Agovino's first book lead you wrong. *The Bookmaker* does contain a running account of his father's avocation as a bet taker and maker, but there's not the inside-look at organized crime that you might expect. In fact, this memoir is more about how a kid like Agovino grew up in New York Co-Op City housing up in the Bronx and into a journalist who could make the book his father never could.

This is the story of how an Italian-American family lived a pretty normal life in a very abnormal environment. Ugo Agovino, Michael's father, was born in Italian Harlem. He forget to make a bet that would have won its maker thousands and had to hide out for a while. Hugo, as he is called, returns to the neighborhood, finds a wife of Sicilian immigrants, and together they become one of the first (and the few Italian) families to move into the city's post-Cold War answer to working-class housing.

Co-Op, a large development of high-rises and town homes built on landfill was home to the Agovino's for twenty-four years, and throughout that time there was not a day when his mother didn't wish she lived elsewhere. The move begins in optimism: "This is a land of promise. A new start, a new beginning, a tabula rasa, a future, a salvation," and ends with car thefts, muggings, and beatings. This is a story of struggle, survival, and hopes for a better life—father and mother try to build on the inside of their kids' lives in spite of the failure of urban renewal.

Ugo maintains a city job that alone does not provide for

the family, and so he resorts to his early experience as a private bookmaker who takes care of those gentlemen gamblers who can afford to lose a little bit here and there. The problem is not in the bet taking, but the bad bet making that Ugo does. When times are good, Ugo, an avid reader and a dedicated consumer of classy stuff like music, fine wines, great works of art and literature tries to treat his family like royalty. Before he's twenty years old, the Agovinos have traveled throughout Europe, to the Caribbean and Latin America—sometimes with enough money to afford a "good bottle of Bordeaux," often with not enough money to pay the hotel bill.

If not always on time, Hugo manages to pay all bills that put his kids through good schools, giving them a better start on adulthood than he might have had, despite putting them through the ups and downs of his own gambling, which he stops after his business peters out.

What makes *The Bookmaker* good reading, is not the very ordinary story of the Agovinos but Michael's extraordinary way of telling it. Style trumps substance here, and when he doesn't maintain the beat and pace of the early chapters, Agovino risks losing readers through occasional telling litanies of themes like what he did during school trips and summer days in the projects during the 1970s and 80s. Fortunately these sections are more lapses than lacunae. By the time you're done with the book you find yourself rooting for the family and feel good that while they never achieved that American dream of owning their own home, the Agovinos have accomplished that rare goal of having shaped a unique history full of interesting stories.

Made up of memories, research, and family interviews, *The Bookmaker* is a testament to how a different kind of Italian American upbringing can lead to the creation of a typical American story.

B. Amore
An Italian American Odyssey (New York: CMS Press)
ISBN: 978-1577030461
August 2007

In 2000 the art of B. Amore inhabited six of the original dormitory rooms of the Ellis Island Immigration museum in a temporary exhibit called "Life line—filo della vita". Those rooms were filled with Amore's artistic responses to her family's immigration from Italy, which included photographs, documents, everyday objects, writings, sculpture, oral histories, installations and video.

Each piece contributed to the puzzle of more than one hundred years of her family's presence in the U.S. Experiencing the art was a journey in itself. From the moment you entered the space you had the sense that this exhibit was unique and that you had to work to get through it all.

That exhibit left New York and traveled to Boston, Rome and Naples in an interesting reverse migration that expanded viewers' ideas of the effects of turn-of-the century immigration. Now, six years after the first showing, that experience has been captured on the page in a beautifully produced coffee-table book.

The keys to the book's success are the crisp and clear illustrations of the artwork that appeared in the exhibit. Amore has trapped that three-dimensional wonder in whole and in details with precise photographs creating a portable museum of sorts. You have to see the beauty of it all to believe it. Amore has taken great pains to make sure that the essence of the exhibit survives this move to the flat page.

More than anything, this book is about the value of holding on to the past and transforming it into something useful for the present. This comes through quite clearly in her great-great-grandfather's "Libro di Memorie," an 1802 handwritten diary that brought her into an awareness of a reality too few of us have ever accessed. Her work extends beyond her family as she records pieces of the histories of those she encountered through research and along the way to making and presenting the exhibit.

At the heart of the exhibit is the life and work of Amore's maternal grandmother, Concettina, who was one of eleven Italian immigrant women in higher education back in the early 1900s. Concettina left behind school notebooks along with the work objects of her profession as a designer/dressmaker that Amore has turned into magnificent pieces of art.

Amore adds a sometimes ironic, but always aesthetically pleasing, touch to the presentation of the materials, providing a wonderful lesson in how to honor and criticize a culture at the same time. The creation experience was transformative, as Amore writes: "It is actually through making the work that I discover myself and my roots more profoundly. They reveal themselves unexpectedly through dark, densely packed soil which I am excavating in the seemingly slowest of ways, digging by hand, a small bit at a time, until a gnarled node is unearthed almost without my knowing, but the light catches it and shows me the way forward."

Besides the exhibit, the book contains commentaries by some of the leading scholars in Italian American studies. The most intense essay is a Supplement by Pellegrino D'Acierno called "Bricolage Blues: Fragments for B. Amore's Life line — filo della vita" that shows how the exhibit impacted his own life and the world outside the museum.

The English is all translated into Italian in the back of the book, which makes it accessible to Italians. The book is available in hardcover and paperback, but I suggest you do yourself a favor. Drop the few extra dollars for the hardcover edition. A book like this is one for the generations.

John Andreozzi

The Italians of Lackawanna, NY: Steelworkers, Merchants and Gardeners
    (Shoreview, MN)
ISBN: 0-9728945-2-7
March 2013

Why should anyone outside of Lackawanna, New York want to read this book? This was the first question I faced when John Andreozzi's five pounds of local history arrived on my desk. I haven't seen such a massive book in a long time. In this day of short attention spans, *The Italians of Lackawanna, New York*, defies not only what one expects to find in bookstores, but also what you might expect to find in an author. And by the time I got through all 673 pages, my answer could only be this: everyone who is interested in Italian American culture needs to take this book seriously as a new model for local studies.

"Over 16 years in the making," as the back cover states, this incredibly detailed study uses local history and story to reach beyond the neighborhood of the author's birth to touch the lives of every Italian American. In it you will find a great deal of information about the upstate New York town of immigrants from over 92 countries that grew into a city that inspired James Farley, Chair of the Democratic National Committee in the 1930s, to say, "I'd rather be mayor of Lackawanna than president of the United States," in an interview with Walter Winchell.

What is it about this city (that could never boast of having more than 29,000 residents in any given year) that makes it worth all the time and energy devoted to it by the author? In Andreozzi's hands, Lackawanna becomes a microcosm for Italian America, especially in terms of what happened to the immigrant- and second-generations.

Using a strong interdisciplinary approach, he combines traditional history, oral histories, sociology, ethnography with journalistic interviews and folklore to paint a thorough portrait of the Italian people who called this place their home. This could easily be a textbook in Italian American studies for all of its charts, distillations of major articles in the field of urban and ethnic studies. Combine all this with periodic presentations of his own memories, and you find that there is historical value in the personal and educational value in examining the local. The book is a model for local studies and the proof that studying the local helps you understand the global.

Over 700 illustrations including charts, maps and photos, all of them impeccably reproduced, make this a kind of coffee table book that you can pick up read for a few minutes and return to it regularly. Chapters include Immigration experiences in the late 19th century, assimilation experiences that include the process, rules, and ideals to reveal how acculturation took place and the effects it has on personal and public identities. There are institutional histories of the Catholic Church, work, businesses, unions, social organizations and politics. While all this covers most of what is important in such studies in incredible detail, a weak point is the lack of attention to the arts. Were there artists besides Louis Marrano, musicians other than Larry Covelli? What did these working class pioneers do for fun? Was it all work and no play?

Beyond this gap, there is not much historical turf left unturned by this seasoned scholar who spent years as the archivist of the Order Sons of Italy in America. Unlike other local studies, *The Italians of Lackawanna, NY* spends a great deal of time situating local history in the context of national Italian American culture. The result is one of the most thoroughly documented studies in the field. Complete with subject and name indices, the book will be useful to the professional scholar as well as the amateur and should find its way to personal as well as public libraries.

Tony Ardizzone
The Whale Chaser (Chicago: Academy Chicago Publishers)
ISBN: 978-0-89733-610-9
February 2011

The original whale chaser of American literature was Herman Melville's Ahab of the novel, *Moby Dick*. Like Ahab, Vince Sansone of Tony Ardizzone's latest novel comes from a long line of fishermen; he also suffers a great wound from his past and spends his life trying to heal it in the strangest ways. Unlike Ahab, Sansone comes to terms with his limitations, his fears, and survives.

The Whale Chaser is Sansone's coming-of-age story during the U.S. 1960s and '70s, when old neighborhood identities are obscured by the times that are a changin'. Sansone is the grandson of Italian immigrants who left Italy, settled in San Francisco, and lost their livelihood on the Pacific Ocean to World War II restrictions on enemy aliens. Vito's father becomes a fishmonger in Chicago who takes to selling fish and newspapers in order to make a living. Vince becomes his father's target whenever the old man needs to express his working-class frustrations, since he's the only boy in a family of girls, and he takes off for safety and freedom.

Alternating between Tofino, Canada and Chicago, the story is rich with scenery of the wilderness of British Columbia and the wildness of Chicago's streets. The narration shuffles through Canadian surf and Chicago turf as Sansone wanders from the fish his father feeds his family and the meat his girlfriend's father butchers, to the fisheries and whale watching business in Canada where he has come to hide from his sins. And while he makes immediate material restitution, as a good boy should, it takes him years to find his way to mental health.

In Tofino, Vince begins to find balance, but not before he almost lost himself in the sex, drugs and music of the 1970s. Sansone cultivates weed for a local dealer, offers his home to hitchhikers, and keeps it together through jazz that helps him lose himself "in the spaces between the big, round notes" of great musicians like Ben Webster and Miles Davis. When he befriends a native Indian named Ignatius George, he learns to read the wonders of the land in new ways that keep him healthy and give him the wisdom he needs to survive on his own.

If you lived through the 60s and 70s then you'll know that Ardizzone got it down, and if you didn't you'll learn what it was like. Catholic school education and dances come back to life with vivid scenes of corporal punishment, intellectual rebellion, and cheek-to-cheek slow dancing. When Vince meets Marie Santangelo he never expects that this childhood sweetheart will eventually make him run away from his abusive father and the neighborhood that seems to be suffocating his only chance to be himself. When he turns to one of his buddy's girlfriends for comfort he begins to think that he breaks everything he touches.

Ardizzone has a knack of saying out loud the things you've always felt, but could never put into words, as in Vince's meditations on meat sauce: "When the history of food in the New World is written, some astute researcher will record the importance of pork neckbones to Midwest American's children from Southern Italy. Take an impoverished population deprived of meat, expose them to an inexpensive and plentiful source, and watch them use it to transform one of their most cherished dishes . . . .pasta cu sugu . . . ."

Sin, redemption, death and resurrection—Ardizzone's story goes deep into the 1960s and '70s to tell a tale worthy of our attention and worth our time. Like the power of good jazz, this novel creates original riffs and a story that's unique.

Helen Barolini

A Circular Journey (New York: Fordham University Press)
ISBN: 0-8232-2615-8
January 2007

I've always admired the writing of Helen Barolini, who is one of Italian America's most important artists. She's written novels (*Umbertina* and *Love in the Middle Ages*, short stories *More Italian Hours*, essays *Chiaroscuro*, and poems, but for many years was known for her work as an editor and translator of her husband's writing. The young Helen Mollica, dreamed of marrying a poet and being one her self. Steeped in the study of Latin at the convent school that had educated her mother—a child of immigrants from Calabria, and a descendant of Sicilian immigrants on her father's side, Helen was better prepared to travel to Virgil's Italy when she completed college than the homeland of her ancestors. She couldn't speak a word of Italian, yet felt she had to be there.

In Italy Helen was introduced to the journalist and poet, Antonio Barolini, they fell in love as she taught him English and he taught her Italian, and they soon after married. Little did Helen know that by marrying a poet, especially a successful, Italian one, that her parents would think she had regressed in their attempts to Americanize their family. She also had to face the fact that her own work would have to wait decades while she played the dutiful wife and mother, raising three daughters and supporting one poet by providing for his home and English audience. They were able to live both in Italy and the U.S. until his sudden death in 1971. Out of the grief of a love lost, Barolini was able to exercise her independence and her writer's voice. The result was over thirty years of an independent writer's life out of which she fashioned a unique voice and a permanent, award-winning place in the history of American letters.

The stories of these years come through fifteen essays she's collected in her latest book, *A Circular Journey*. In each section, "Home," "Abroad" and "Return" are essays that mark spiritual stages of her life. The early essays present information about her childhood, most of which took place on a street named after the father of the famous writer Henry James. Here we learn of the experiences that created a writer's imagination. The middle section recounts her life abroad, mostly with Antonio and Italy's post-World War II major writers' circle, which included Nobel Prize winners like Eugenio Montale. And the final section brings us to the words of a seasoned writer who is finally at home, not only in her country of birth, but in her writer's self. She has lived to be the writer she was afraid she might have lost earlier in her life.

Barolini has always proven to be a first-rate essay writer, and I've always thought that was where she has done her best work. Most of the essays succeed because she easily balances the punch of an editorial writer with the poise of a poet. At times sections border on travelogues, but because she is so adept at describing her surroundings we don't feel we're watching home movies. If you read the essays in order, you might be bothered by some of the repetition, but no more so than if you were listening to a good storyteller tell the same story over again. You don't mind it because there's always something new in the way it's told that carries you along. And after all, Barolini is one of the best life story tellers we have today, one we might just call our First Lady of Italian American literature.

Gina Barreca

It's Not that I'm Bitter . . . or How I learned to Stop Worrying about Visible Panty Lines and Conquered the World (New York: St. Martin's Press)
ISBN: 978-0-312-54726-4
April 2010

Gina Barreca cracks me up. If you haven't had the chance to read or see her act, you can pick up her latest book, *It's Not that I'm Bitter...or How I learned to Stop Worrying about Visible Panty Lines and Conquered the World*, and taste her humor, much of which has previously appeared in magazines and journals.

Author and editor of nearly 20 books, mostly of or about humor, Barreca is a regular columnist and contributor to a number of publications, including *The Philadelphia Inquirer*, *The Hartford Courant*, *Education World*, *The Chronicle of Higher Education* and more; she is also professor of English at the University of Connecticut.

Barreca is the consummate humorist; she's studied it, done it, edited it, written it and about it, historicized it, criticized it, feminized it. Don't read it all at once; savor some and save the rest. Leave it somewhere where you are likely to plop down and take a reading break. You'll find yourself coming back to it whenever you need a smile. She won't be offended if it sits in your restroom or next to your bedtime reading light. One or two of these short pieces every once in a while will have the same effect as two-for-one cocktails at happy hour.

Not every entry is guaranteed to tickle your fancy—many are directed at women, but indirectly she really wants men to read them as well. Pay attention and you'll be privy to a world that Italian men used to call "Chiachera"—woman's talk, but it's like being in the doctor's office and picking up a woman's magazine to see what the latest advice is on how to attract, treat, tantalize, detach or rid yourself of one man or another.

Some of the titles are stand alone humor, such as the essay on reincarnation, "If You Don't Pay Your Exorcist Do You Get Repossessed?" You get the sense that Barreca can find the humor in anything, and she does. Feminism, dating, Christmas, buying bras, bathing suits, what women wear, hear, see, become when they are with each other, around men, at work, at home, it seems she's got her eye everywhere, searching for that scene that will help you laugh your way into understanding that you are weird and that you are not alone.

There's a fair bit of humor about being Italian, but as with other contemporary comedians, she doesn't' stray far from her experiences with her family, well represented in "Who's Funnier", an essay focusing on the difference between men and women.

"My big Italian family was funny. And we were poor, which is why I am comfortable saying the poor are funnier than the rich. You had to be funny in our neighborhood or else you couldn't survive; you had to learn to "crack wise," to make yourself heard about the sound of your aunt Josephine whacking a cutlet with a wooden mallet like John Henry laying down track. If our humor was vulgar—bathroom humor, slyly suggestive sexual innuendo or the irreverent mocking of the social norms—well, that's because we were basically prototypes for The Vulgar."

She is as seriously funny as she is serious about the role humor plays in being a human. "By seeing the ironies and absurdities of the world around us we can lighten up and be less weighed down—humor permits perspective, and perspective is essential for change." *It's Not That I'm Bitter . . .* takes on the heavy topics such as aging, health, gender equity, and history, instilling in every one a perspective that you might have had your self or, most likely, never considered.

If you'd like to know more about her and keep up with her many writings and appearances you can check out her website at www.ginabarreca.com

Joseph Bathanti

The Life of the World to Come (Columbia, SC: University of South Carolina Press)
ISBN: 978-1-6117-453-3
August 2014

We all come from one East Liberty or another. It's a familiar place that gets richer as time moves on. It's that place that memory fuses out of fact and fantasy, out of what was and what should have been—the place where imagination takes what once was real and weaves it into something that's useful. The pieces of our personal history that come from such places become the building blocks of personality, and for the fiction writer, that past becomes a playground out of which stories, often better than the histories, are spun.

East Liberty, Pennsylvania, a working-class neighborhood of Pittsburgh, has been the setting for much of the fiction and some of the poetry of Joseph Bathanti. His first novel, about to be reprinted, was in fact entitled *East Liberty*. In his latest novel, *The Life of the World to Come*, Bathanti returns to his birthplace to set in motion all the things that can turn a good boy bad.

George Dolce, a kid born to working-class parents—both children of Italian immigrants—is a smart, hardworking college kid who gambles just enough to help his family out. His bets, for the most part are smart and safe, and designed to get him through college and into an Ivy League law school. When he takes a job at the local pharmacy, run by Mr. Rosechild, a Jewish man who has money to burn and a loyalty to his home team, the Pittsburgh Steelers, George hones in on his bookie's business, taking the pharmacist for the money he needs to keep his family from in their home when his father loses his job.

The worse happens after George falls in love with Rosechild's daughter, and the pharmacist's betting gets out of hand. George gets in trouble with his bookie, which means he also must deal with the local gangster who runs things in the hood. The result is a tragic story of a young man's fall from grace and his futile flight toward freedom.

Throughout the novel, George narrates what happens as well as what could happen. The result is a narrative tension that keeps the reader wondering how it's all going to end. Bathanti, a poet as well as a natural-born story teller, casts a literary crime story that becomes part thriller, part coming-of-age account of something that could happen to any smart kid who tries too hard to fight what he perceives could be the fate of following in his father's hopeless footsteps.

East Liberty is a place where even the best of the local kids end up on its skid-row streets. We see it all first, as George gives his middle-class girlfriend a tour of the neighborhood in her father's Cadillac, and later, as George turns into Michael Roman and walks Crow, his new girlfriend, through East Liberty's tough streets as he tries to make good all the bad he's done. While it's too late to change the past, George hopes it's not too late to save his soul.

Somewhere between George's fantasies and the narrator's reality lies the magic makes this novel a must read. This tale of two Georges, crafted by a master of the literary trade, reminds us that literature can still do more than any film to reveal the extremes humanity can handle when facing the obstacles we all face when trying to realize our dreams.

Restoring Sacred Art: Poetry (Scottsdale, AZ: Star Cloud Press)
ISBN: 978-1-932842-40-1
June 2012

When's the last time you actually stopped to read a poem? I don't mean those short, rarely witty tweets that come through one of your electronic connections to the world, or those song lyrics that sometimes get mistaken for rhyme. I mean a real honest-to-goodness poem, something that made you think differently about life after you read it. If it's been a while since you've had that kick in the forehead that Jack Kerouac used to call satori, or enlightenment, then take a look a Joseph Bathanti's latest collection of poems.

There is no doubt in my mind that Joseph Bathanti is one of the finest writers Italian America has produced, and one of the few that can be considered good enough to make it into American canonical literature. Whether it's through poetry, the novel or short fiction, Bathanti has a way of latching onto a character or an idea and not letting go until he gets you to care about his protagonists, even if you don't like them. You know them, and he reminds you of that. He writes in a way that makes reading seem effortless. His diction never calls attention to itself and always sounds real. All of his best comes through in his latest collection of poems.

Bathanti, who has won awards with nearly every one of his previous publications (five books of poetry, two novels, and a book of short fiction), takes us through a lifetime of experiences and the memories of growing up and out of a Little Italy in Pittsburgh, Pennsylvania in his new book, *Restoring Sacred Art*. The poet turns everyday experiences into the sacred by remembering and creating a means by which to capture it.

Some of his poems can be read as secular prayers that reach into worlds beyond the present to make new connections to the past. Everyday objects become relics that release stories in the way the poets review them. A neighborhood pick-up ballgame turn into a fight and is captured by the poet in slow motion scenes that turns a boy's first confession into a reminder that sin never sleeps after he punches Jacky, "a bad angel" who then "soughed a crown of blood at my feet."

Each poem is a cameo story formed of priests, nuns, family and local neighbors who are reborn into glory through the poet's words, a glory that can only be awarded by those who's memory is captured in art. The mysteries learned through Catholic education become the stuff for many of the poems, and many of the lessons learned become stories about the teachers and students who taught each other how to negotiate the daily challenges of faith, hope and charity.

The story of a school's janitor whose horrible death while drunk evokes the torture of martyrs gets its title from "Face of Fire," a 1959 "B" movie and elevates this common man's story into a town legend. When a young boy uses a swear word for the first time in his mother's presence, he watches as she "backed mutely/ into her room and out of my life—/ As if she were about to crash unclothed/ through the window into the snowstorm,/ leaving me once and for all."

The petty crimes and childhood sins of shoplifting, fist-fighting, swearing become the stuff of some memorable poems. The rigors of training for high school wrestling, parents aging, love aching, hearts fluttering on first dates, all make their way into stories captured in verse that whispers poetry and shouts familiarity. When you find yourself in one of these poems you'll smile at the way some stranger has captured your feelings with his words.

The High Heart (Cheney, WA: Eastern Washington University Press)
ISBN: 978-1-59766-033-4
November 2008

Joseph Bathanti's latest publication, *The High Heart*, is another winner in a history of strong writing that includes four books of poetry and the Carolina Novel Award winning "East Liberty". He's won many other awards including a 2002 Sherwood Anderson Award. So if you don't know him yet, his latest work is a good place to start.

Set in Pittsburgh in the 1960s and 1970s, this cycle of fourteen stories surrounds the nuclear family of Travis, Rita and their son Frederick "Fritz" Sweeney. Travis works as a waiter in a high-class restaurant, Rita, a hostess in a club, where Fritzy wonders if she's a stripper, and Fritz, who is in that painful and exciting period of transition from high school to life on one's own.

His parents are not the Cleavers. They work nights, come home long after they've hit the afterhours bars, and then wake up in the afternoon, sometimes with enough time to see their only child. Rita often thinks about having another child and in the stories "Thy Womb Jesus" and "Zeppole" we learn that it might not be a good idea, as she might just be certifiably crazy. Yet, this craziness is something that father and son have learned how to deal with and so we wonder if it could just be us, less tolerable because we are less experienced, who are living life differently. And this is the joy of reading Bathanti. He challenges the extraordinary by focusing on the very ordinary lives of his characters.

The stories cover the usual coming-of-age themes such as family, work, school, sex and love, but the Bathanti difference is this risk he takes in diving deeper into issues such as sports participation so that we see just what it takes to become a "macho wrestler". One of the longest stories is "The School for the Blind," in which Fritz takes us through his experience as a wrestler in high school. From his exercise, diet and exploits, he survives and then comes the meet when they must wrestle kids who are blind. The coach prepares them by having them walk around blindfolded, funny, high school antics, and bouts of bulimia that help him make weight for his matches.

When Fritz graduates high school, but has no idea what he wants to do so he goes to work for his mother's brother, a job his father had once tried and couldn't handle. In no time, Fritz is caught between his mother's expectations and his father's fears. He carries hod for bricklayers like Shotty Montesanto who teaches him how to do everything but stay on a scaffold. Shotty comes back to us in a few stories, most notably in "Scaffold" and "Decoration Day," and we wonder will Fritz ever make it out of this world in which the pain of everyday work is soothed only by every night substance abuse.

Bathanti writes in a way that makes reading seem effortless. His diction never calls attention to itself and always sounds real. The stories can be read all at once as though it was a long movie, or independently as if you could lift individual frames out of the whole. Either way, either the beauty of the language or the wisdom in the story will get you to read many of these more than once.

Marcella Bencivenni
Italian Immigrant Radical Culture: The Idealism of the Sovversivi in the United States, 1890-1940 (New York: New York University Press)
ISBN: 978-0-8147-9103-5.
December 2011

Building on the ground breaking work of those who came before her, Marcella Bencivenni, an assistant professor of history at Hostos Community College of the City University of New York, has written a thorough and compelling account of the Italian contribution to American working class history. Bencivenni's *Italian Immigrant Radical Culture: The Idealism of the Sovversivi in the United States, 1890-1940* builds on the work of historians such as Rudolf Vecoli, Nunzio Pernicone, Salvatore Salerno, Donna Gabaccia and Jennifer Guglielmo, to create an original work that is essential reading for anyone in American cultural history.

I have read many accounts of Italian radicalism in the United States, but Bencivenni's is unlike any other to date. The writing is lively, clear and fluid. It's virtually jargonless, making it accessible to the readers beyond the usual academic community while being extremely useful to the veteran scholar. The tight focus of her study of fifty years of American history enables her to examine Italian American culture in depth and reach across ethnic issues to connect to the larger story of America's working class life and culture. She does this by presenting both the political and the socio-cultural aspects of Italian immigrant radicals, "the way traditions, institutions, literature, and art fused with and sustained political work," as she writes in her "Introduction".

In her first chapter, "Italian American Radicalism, Old World Roots, New World Developments," Bencivenni tells the story of immigration and discusses the impact Italian intellectuals and workers had on early labor movements. She makes the point that Italians participated in many strikes and brought "new elements of struggle into the American labor movement" such as moving picket lines, the "children's exodus" (during the Lawrence Strike of 1912, and when necessary, they we not afraid to return the violence they received.

"The Sovversivi and Their Cultural World," explores the world that created Italian American radicals and pays close attention to the development of radical thought and action among the women. Through reading groups, lecture tours, alternative education, dances and feste (such as May Day), the "sovversivi" educated each other and changed old world-thinking into new world actions that ennobled former peasants and enabled them to confront the forces of oppression. Their ideas were shaped and sustained through various news and literary publications.

Chapter Three, "A Literary Class War" takes a close look at the press and periodical publications. Riccardo Cordiferro referred to the worker's goal as "the conquest of the book", and these "conquests" not only fostered new political thinking, but also new ways of living in the United States that would unite the working class and guide them toward better lives.

In "Politics and Leisure," Bencivenni focuses on the role that theater played in educating and entertaining the workers, pointing out that "stage was not 'just' a weapon in the class struggle; it also reflected the artistic needs of the 'sovversivi'". Her next chapter, "Italian American Literary Radicalism," takes us beyond previous surveys to present an overview of the great amount of activity that took place in the fiction and poetry created by such writers as Simplicio Righi, Antonino Crivello, Riccardo Cordiferro, Bellalma Forzato-Spezia, Virgilia D'Andrea and many others. This survey is followed by comprehensive chapters on two important figures, poet and organizer Arturo Giovannitti and cartoonist Fort Velona.

A brief conclusion explains how this amazing energy disappeared and offers us much to think about in terms of how Italian immigrant radicalism affected Americanization of the Italian immigrant.

Adria Bernardi
Openwork (Dallas, TX: Southern Methodist University Press)
ISBN: 978-0-87074-510-2
March 2008

Many writers have told the story of Italian immigration to the United States that sometimes I get the feeling that it's all been done and there's nothing new to say. Then along comes a writer who through a rich use of language and a sharp sense of structure creates a whole new way of seeing things. That writer is Adria Bernardi, and in her new novel, *Openwork*, she captures the intergenerational impact of immigration so well and with such a literary flair that she has given us a story that transcends the burden of history.

Bernardi's new work comes after a history of Italians in her hometown of Highwood, IL, and two award winning books of fiction: a collection of stories, *In the Gathering Woods*, and the novel *The Day Laid on the Altar*. The new novel's title refers to a type of needlework stitch that enables you to see through what the cloth covers, and is an apt metaphor for the story. Various narrators try to create meaning out of their own and their ancestors out of the pieces of history and story they accumulate. The result is a literary openwork in which insight gained by one sometimes does and sometimes doesn't reach the next generation; what we don't know often becomes the empty space that leaves us with as many questions as answers.

Openwork is divided into three parts. The first builds a sense of the Italian families in Italy through Imola Bartolai Martinelli, a housewife and needle worker, who is willing do to what she needs to do to help her family thrive in the mountains of Northern Italy even if it means risking the comfort of her own children. Imola, in many ways, serves as the foundation of most of the stories that follow. Through her children, and the friends and families they make, we come to know three generations of Italian Americans and the lives that they have fashioned out of the immigrant experience in places like Colorado, New Mexico, and Chicago. The second part takes place in Highwood, Illinois and the characters from part one are now grandparents. The final section focuses on one grandchild, Adele, a rather precocious and intelligent child who grows up trying to make sense of her family history.

There's nothing highly dramatic in this novel, but the way Bernardi renders the ordinary, everyday aspects of life makes it a compelling read. Sure there are exciting scenes of mountain travel, a mining disaster, a precarious drive through a tough Chicago neighborhood, but what happens in the mind of each character transcends what happens to the body. You will feel this novel as you read it, and when you've finished you will be full, as though you've had an excellent meal.

Readers familiar with literary theory might catch the echo of *The Open Work* by Umberto Eco in the way Bernardi has woven an open-ended tale out of the bits and pieces of family history that come to us from many perspectives, and in the way she enables a number of interpretations to be validated out of the information she provides from various points-of-view. This is an invisible force that elevates the novel beyond memory-based fiction and into the realm of true literary art. *Openwork* fulfills the promise of her earlier fiction, and establishes Bernardi as a serious and seasoned storyteller whose way with words makes reading a pleasure.

Giorgio Bertellini

Italy in Early American Cinema: Race, Landscape, and the Picturesque (Bloomington, IN: Indiana University Press)
ISBN: 978-0-253-22128-5
August 2010

Professor Giorgio Bertellini has become known as an expert in early Italian and American cinema through his many articles that have appeared both in Italy and the U.S. His new book is a magisterial work that finds its strength by connecting his studies of art, photography, cinema and video, creating a unique sense of the development of racial and national identities.

Bertellini painstakingly builds connections between landscape art and cinema to move beyond tradition cinema studies that have focused solely on aesthetic or sociological phenomena. By connecting these fields, Bertellini helps us to see how ideas introduced in earlier media are reworked through subsequent media developments; the result is that we are made aware of how what have seemed to be a cultural rupture is sometimes simply a repetition or a reintroduction of an already familiar image through an unfamiliar new medium. These connections are solidly placed in a well-developed argument.

Bertellini does in this book what no one prior has done in Italian American cinema studies, he examines the ways in which ethnic and mainstream cinema was consumed and reacted to by the immigrants themselves and presents evidence that Italian immigrants were agents as well as subjects of their own representation. The argument here is meticulous and based on incredibly detailed evidence that often comes from never-before consulted archival materials. He makes an excellent case for the way Roman antiquity impacted the politics and national identities of emerging nations during the 18th and 19th centuries. His work here is especially useful for anyone dealing with the way stereotypes are fashioned and employed in the assertion of national identities. Anyone who has worked on the gangster image in American culture (such as myself) needs to reconsider previous work in light of Bertellini's take on the role of the "banditi," "briganti," and "mafiosi" in early photography, art and cinema.

Certainly the foundation for the American reception of the gangster figure lies in what Bertellini has uncovered and explored through the figures of the "briganti" and "banditi" as opposed to the cowboys of "Western" films as many critics have argued. His expose of "racial masquerading" will shed light on the way stereotypes are reified, commoditized, and analyzed in American studies. This is an original discovery that will no doubt impact the study of stereotypes in U.S. media. His argument, that "Racialness...defined American cinema more than it did any other Western film culture" is well structured, documented, and challenges previous studies of American cinema in ways that will no doubt impact future work in this area.

With this book, Bertellini has become a scholar who must be recognized and reckoned with by all future students and scholars in the field of immigrant cultural studies.

His work here uncovers a lost link between immigrants and their progeny, a link that has been missed by nearly all previous scholars who have not examined Italian language productions. Today's Italian American cannot know this past, this tradition unless they have first learned the language(s) in which the work was conceived and executed and then taken the time to study that work. Bertellini has done a great service not just to the Italian American citizen, but also to the American film scholar by concentrating on this overlooked, but rich vein of American culture.

Mary Jo Bona
By the Breath of Their Mouths (Albany, NY: SUNY Press)
ISBN: 978-1-4384-2996-0
October 2010

Mary Jo Bona, Professor of Italian American Studies at Stony Brook University, and the chairperson of the Women's and Gender Studies Program, is renowned for her teaching, scholarship and poetry. She's published essays and critical studies that have become must reading in the field of Italian American studies. She's directed graduate students, edits a book series at SUNY press, has directed the Italian American Studies Program at Stony Brook and is Past-President of the American Italian Historical Association. It's hard to find anyone as committed as she is to the field of American multicultural studies and Italian American Studies in particular, and now she has brought the best of her experiences and knowledge to bear in a new book.

By the Breath of Their Mouths: Narratives of Resistance in Italian America is Bona's latest publication, a unique study of Italian American literature old and new. She uses a thematic approach that focuses on issues of justice, faith, storytelling, land, history, influence, death and revival. Through this work she builds a bridge to the next phase of Italian American literary criticism — the integration of Italian American writings into the U.S. canon.

The entire work is pedagogically sound. Whether you are reading the novels for the first time or teaching them for the tenth, you find insights here that will take you beyond your own thinking to new levels of perception. The elegant, careful style of writing is erudite without being opaque. Each essay is constructed through rigorously informed criticism, the result of working and rehearsing ideas for years before putting them down on the page, of testing those ideas in conference presentations, public lectures, and classrooms, distilling those experiences into wisdom appearing in the written word.

"Acts of writing ensured Italian Americans of at least two things: that they would not forget an ancestral heritage replete with communal and inclusive storytelling traditions; and that assimilation in American could be deflected by recording and establishing resistant voices in narratives expressive of folk practices and family cultures. "

Justice, the relation of private justice to the folklore traditions found in the writings of Pietro di Donato, Mari Tomasi, Jerre Mangione, Tina DeRosa, and Tony Ardizzone

Her essay on faith brings us new teaks on women and Catholicism, confessing, and outing with interpretations leading to insights such as, "Italian American authors have regularly developed characters whose brand of Catholicism—unorthodox at best—requires them to function in a doubly marginalized way—as Italian American Catholics and as Italian American citizens."

If you had ever thought Italian American literature doesn't matter then doubt no more as Mary Jo Bona with her mastery of the history and criticism of U.S. American literature demonstrates the centrality and vitality of this vein of the American literary goldmine. This is done best in her chapter on the writer Guido D'Agostino, which is co-written by one of her graduate students JoAnne Ruvoli. The co-authors sees D'Agostino's attempts to contribute to U.S. literature as allow[ing] him to discover echoes of his soul, which also remained tied to his parents' ancestral homeland—Sicily." You don't have to lose your roots in order to become American, and you don't have to write about your roots to be an Italian American writer.

Her style of comparative reading exacts readings of such writers as Tina DeRosa and the Barbadian/American writer, Paule Marshall that invigorate the field. She examines intracultural influences by applying that approach to her readings of Louise DeSalvo with Mary Cappello, and Maria Gillan with Rose Romano.

Her chapter on death explains much about the way Italian Americans see their lives and the deaths of those they love in the context of their cultural history. She concludes with a finale that would easily become the prelude to the next important study of Italian American literature.

Bernard J. Bruno
A Tear and a Tear in the Heart (New York: Bordighera Press)
ISBN: 978-1-59954-081-8
December 2014

You think you know someone; you think you know your past and those who played a part in shaping it. And all that thinking creates memories that you hold dear and return to now and then for comforting reminders of how good it once was. Then you meet someone from your past and as you recount shared memories you realize there was more to what happened than your perspective, and that new knowledge will forever change the way you see that past.

This is what will happen to you when you read Barney Bruno's collection of memoirs: *A Tear and A Tear in My Heart*. This collection of real-life stories are set in Melrose Park, Illinois, but could the location could be Anywhere, USA. Bruno's observations on his over ninety years of life in Melrose Park from childhood through his retirement years cover a range of public and private experiences that bring out the best and worst of our common humanity.

From his early days as a young lawyer whose clients included some of the most notorious gangsters of our times, to his legal encounters with the Melrose hoi polloi of the 1940s through the 1990s, Bruno reveals his role in such feats as uncovering and breaking the illegal baker's union that once put stamps on loaves of bread, standing up to Bobby Kennedy's bullying of innocent people, and the many ways in which he assisted those who needed protection by and from the law. Throughout it all he maintains a distance from his subjects that bring out an uncommon authority that is hard to achieve when writing memoirs.

Though some of his stories might be familiar to those who live in the localities of which he writes, most of us never knew as much as Barney, and so he fills important background gaps that enrich the stories we have heard, enlightening us with new ways of seeing old experiences. Here we have not only the realizations of the mythical American dream, but also the failures behind the successes, something that has been missing in traditional histories, especially of Italian America.

Bruno explores working-class life and work as they come into contact with uses and abuses of the rich and raw passions of those who longed to make a place for themselves and their families in the new land. His take on the evolution of organized crime in Chicago, "In Da 'Heyday,'" is a simple and sober retelling of the facts behind the mythic "Outfit," and works quite well when followed by "From Italian to American," "Guts Sans Glory," and a number of tales of Villa Scalabrini to reveal a wider range of heroic Italian behavior than we normally get from such stories.

Take these stories for what they are, one man's attempt to mark the time he has spent living in a Chicago suburb as a lawyer for the poor and the powerful; through it all he remained as calm and stable, and he tells it all with the peace that comes with a long life. He has been like the eye in the middle of a strong storm, a witness to the power of nature and to the will of humans to survive all that they face. He calls this collection A Tear in the Heart, for pain and compassion are two sides of the same coin we call life.

Mary Bucci Bush
Sweet Hope (Toronto: Guernica Editions)
ISBN: 978-1-55071-342-8
April 2012

In *Sweet Hope*, Mary Bucci Bush, turns her attention to a great historical void: the story of Italian American life on southern plantations during the early 1900s. Though they were called Italian colonies, to which Italians were shipped directly from Italy, many were little more than new versions of slavery. Bush's grandmother had gone to the south when she was seven years old. Though this was a common experience, very little has been published about it. Fueled by her grandmother's stories, Bush found that Blacks and Italians lived next door to each other, in separate plantation shacks, and socialized with each other.

This is a novel that I have been expecting for a long time. Portions of it have previously appeared in anthologies and a chapbook, and finally it has all come together in *Sweet Hope*. The author's research into her family's immigration to the south has turned into a story that rivals the best of Toni Morrison's tales of life in America's early 20th century south as Italian immigrants moved in to fill the absence caused by the flight of former slaves.

Based on actual experiences in the Sunnyside Plantation of Arkansas, *Sweet Hope* dramatizes a reality that is never mentioned in U.S. history books, and should cause all Italian Americans to reconsider the privileges of being white in a country founded on racism. Bush focuses on two families, one black—the Halls, one Italian—the Pascalas, who reluctantly turn to each other for help in making their way on an inhumane plantation run by a rogue manager fronting for the owner who is an aspiring politician trying to keep his distance from the unfair treatment of his tenant farmers and the economic prison in which he has them trapped.

Bush captures the daily life struggles, loves, lies, friendship and fears shared and deferred of Italian and African American families.

Old fashioned American racism comes to the surface through the interactions of the children; one, named Isola, is the daughter of Italian immigrants, the other, Birdie, is the daughter of freed-black slaves who have become sharecroppers. In the following passage, Isola divulges a secret that identifies a key tension in this historical fiction:

> "My mother says we all have to watch out now," Isola told
> Birdie. Maybe the Americans make more trouble for us if they see us playing with the Sant'Angelos [a troubled family]." She lowered her voice. If we play with Nina the Americans will shoot us."
> Birdie took a step back and looked at Isola. "Where you got such a crazy idea?"
> "That's what Mr. Gates' men do," Isola said. "That's what my Papa told me."
> Birdie put her hand on her hips. "You dumb or something? White folks don't shoot white folks." She walked faster, so that Isola had to trot to catch up with her.
> "But we're not white," Isola told her. "We're Italian." (228)

This distinction, between Italian and white, has never before been dramatized with such power and precision in American fiction.

The prose is compelling and the narrative never lags. Bush is a master at moving the story along through dialogue that captures the cadences of Black and Italian dialects. The novel is filled with twists and turns that take us through the trials of socially forbidden relationships and actions that turn strangers into friends and friends into family. In the end, the novel becomes a great awakening to the realities of a past that has been hidden, speaking to a present that will benefit through such awareness.

Dierdre Marie Capone
Uncle Al Capone (Boston: Recap Publishing Company)
ISBN: 978-0982845103
September 2011

Most of what we know of Al Capone was written by people who didn't know him. News—and soon afterwards, fictional accounts—of his criminal exploits flooded mass media, creating an insatiable appetite for anything Capone. The legend grew faster than Capone could work, creating a superman that no lawman could stop. A mock trial held by the American Bar Association Litigation Section at the 1991 ABA annual meeting acquitted Capone after retrying the case with the original 1931 evidence.

Capone-mania lasted so long that Geraldo Rivera jumped into it, devoting a whole television show to breaking into a vault supposedly containing Capone's hidden loot, and turning up nothing but empty bottles and dust. If like Rivera, you're looking for more Capone dirt, you won't find it here; in fact, what Deidre gives you will make you think twice about what is true and false about the man everyone thinks they know.

Dierdre is the daughter of Ralph Capone, Jr., the son of Al's brother. Ralph, Jr. was a smart kid and his father made sure he had every educational advantage that he hadn't had back when he and Al were roaming the streets of Brooklyn. Ralph went from prep school to college to law school, graduating tops in all his classes. When it came time for him to practice law, the Bar Association would not allow him in because of his connection to Uncle Al, and after frustrating attempts at legitimate businesses, Ralph supposedly took his own life at the age of 33, leaving Deidre in the care of her divorced mother, her family, and sometimes, the Capones.

Hiding behind her father's middle name, Gabriel, Deirdre tries to make it on her own, but at 17, she loses her first big job because her company found out the name on her birth certificate. From here on, Deirdre's story is one in which she find trouble in the world that is comforted, if not solved, by her Capone aunts and uncles. She only knew Al for a few years, but her memories are many and fond.

Written as a book for family members, as a way of making peace with the turmoil her family name caused her, *Uncle Al Capone*, is a tolerable first memoir, written out of necessity for all the right reasons. She's not cashing in on the name that almost destroyed her; she's taking us all to places she had to hide when things got tough, and into the lives of the people who saved her along the way.

Carl Capotorto
Twisted Head (Ontario: ExileEditions)
ISBN: 978-0-7679-2861-8
April 2009

When Carl Capotorto's *Twisted Head* arrived on my desk, I was hesitant to touch it. I was afraid I'd encounter a lightweight account of how a kid from the Bronx made it from a pizza joint past to success on the Broadway stage, in independent films, and on national television. What a surprise it was to find that this memoir had life in it as few do.

Capotorto, who simply translated his family name for the title, gives a great account of growing up under a father he loved through fear, a mother who taught him how to put up with men like his father, and sisters who challenged him to defy the status quo of his time and place. Until he learns that he can control his own life, his head is twisted in a number of ways: first, in relation to his family; next, in relation to the boys in the hood who tease, tempt, and taunt him as he finds a way to express his sexuality in New York's late 1970s and '80s disco culture.

What makes *Twisted Head* rise above most other memoirs is Capotorto's ability to write as though he had his arm around your shoulder and was walking you through his neighborhood as he makes it through his fears, foibles, and fantasies. His honesty is refreshing and his insights profound. "My father seems to have been bent on preparing and training me not for life in general, or for the world, but simply for life under his rule, in his house…I wound up being secretly scared of my own shadow well into manhood, insecure and self-conscious to an unbearable degree." He overcomes this fear first through disco dancing, which enables him to create a self in public performance, and then through his pursuit of an artist's life that frees him from his father's pressures as he focuses on playwriting and acting.

There is an intimacy in his prose that avoids in-your-face braggadocio as it takes you through the good and bad times of the Capotorto family. He divides his story into "The Pizza Years" and "The House Years," and both sections are anchored on the work his father does that he draws the young Carl into because he's the only son. Carl becomes his father's helper in a never-ending campaign to rehab the family's house the move into once the pizza business is sold. You can see where he drew from his own life in the creation of Bruno in John Turturro's *Mac* as he deals with his father's demons and demands. The lessons he learns are ones that we must master in some way as we make sense of our own upbringing in the process of creating our identities both inside and outside the family.

The rough life in a pizzeria that barely provides for the family is never depicted as quaint; the disco days transcend the shallowness of *Saturday Night Fever*, and his days in high school and college never reek of nostalgia. Capotorto accomplishes all this by creating an authoritative voice born of hard knocks and deep thinking that surfaces through beautiful language. It's not the story he tells that compels the reader, but the way he writes that keeps the pages turning.

Based on a one-man show Captorto wrote and performed, *Twisted Head* is full of fine stories that speak to a generation of American life that tries to remain connected to ethnic roots while it stretches to become American. By the time you finish *Twisted Head*, you get the feeling that this guy's become a good friend of yours who, while you may have never met him, you will certainly never forget him.

Mary Cappello
Awkward: A Detour (New York: Bellevue Literary Press)
ISBN: 978-1-934137-01-7
April 2008

Mary Cappello, the author of the memoir *Nightbloom*, and professor of English at the University of Rhode Island, has published a new book that is part memoir, part travelogue and part literary and film criticism. You might think that that's a lot to try to get into the book, and that even if you could, making it all fit in and matter to a wide range of readers would result, at best, in something awkward. And it has.

Awkward: A Detour is a collection of meditations on the meaning of awkwardness in an age that ignores most all the most egregious of flaws in the human species. Most awkwardness gets labeled with a caution sign and is avoided. Cappello has taken it on not only as a subject for her writing, but as a way of centering her life. If she's not the queen of awkwardness, then she's certainly a candidate for being its patron saint. Don't take my word for it; check out her website: www.awkwardness.org—she even has a contest for those willing to pursue and present their own awkwardness to the world through video. But back to the book.

If you're looking for a single author in this volume, you'll have a hard time finding her. There are many Mary Cappellos, and some of them are so intelligent they make you jealous, some, so silly you have to laugh, and some so pathetic, that they make you see your own shallowness as they lure you into the depths of self examination that many of us have when we have a good, honest confession.

Whether the subject is her family, her loves, her travels to Italy and Russia, her teaching or writers like Emily Dickinson and Henry James or the filmmaker Werner Fassbinder, Mary has much to say about each and often from more than one perspective. The literary and film criticism might not be so relevant to those who are unfamiliar with the works she examines, but for those who know the works she brings a freshness to criticism that is rare in these days of post-structuralist thought. You've got to wonder at some of the problems that come into her life and the way she tries to solve them, but whatever it may be, she sure knows how to keep her focus on the awkwardness of it all.

In reading this you'll find yourself laughing, sometimes at her and sometimes at yourself, and often at the foolishness found in this life we share with her. Her self-indulgence is at times almost unbearable, but just when you think it's too much, she pulls away from her pathologies and rises to help us see through the guise of self long enough to see the folly of our own fears. This is risky writing, that doesn't always work, but observing that risk at work is what makes *Awkward* worth reading.

"Awkwardness isn't something to grow out of but to grow into," she writes. We need to learn how to become comfortable with all that makes life awkward, and not avoid new possibilities because of fears crafted from past shame. There is no simple way to describe one's own weirdness, but Cappello does it without losing track of her connection to the world. She confronts those acts that many of us have hidden from the world out of a sense of shame cast on us by traditions forged in other time. What she does and the way she does it is unique enough to make this experimental memoir work.

Nancy Carnevale
A New Language, A New World (Champaign, IL)
ISBN: 978-0-25203403-9
January 2011

What does it mean to be an Italian American? Once upon a time that identity depended on knowledge and use of the Italian language. Now that the Italian language is no longer at the core of Italian American identity we've come to depend on other aspects of culture to claim membership. Most Italian Americans know they don't speak language, but they might not know why? And while there are stories in every family, the real answers can be found in Nancy Carnevale's study, *A New Language, A New World: Italian Immigrants in the United States 1890 to 1945*.

Carnevale, an assistant professor of history at Montclair State University in New Jersey, has created a history that joins linguistic based studies of Italian language use by scholars such as Herman Haller, Tullio DeMauro, and Francesco Bruni, to help us understand just what happened when the dialects of Italy met with English.

Her approach is based on a series of problems such as why has so little been done on the history of immigrant languages and their relationships to ethnic identity, and why hasn't immigrant subjectivity been the focus of language studies. The result is a study that "examines key points in the history of Italian immigrants and language in the United Sates, such as the Americanization movement of the early twentieth century and the Second World War" (12) — one that shows us how history has affected the use of the Italian language.

What Carnevale does best is to integrate Italian language use into American history, and she does it in a way that is accessible to the casual reader and informative to the most seasoned scholar. Part One opens with an overview of Italian use in Italy and the United States and a chapter on the role that language use played in the definition of American identity and the practice of American politics. These chapters lay the groundwork for subsequent chapters of Part Two on Italian in translation, the theater, identity politics and the impact of cultural pluralism during World War II.

Part Two begins with a unique look at court records and immigrant autobiographies that reveal how Italian immigrants names were changed (and not by Ellis Island as myths suggest), how poor translations hindered testimonies of witnesses at trials such as the Sacco and Vanzetti, and how immigrants struggled to learn English and often used their situation to their advantage. Carnevale examines autobiographies by immigrants Pascal D'Angelo, Constatine Panunzio, and Rosa Cassetari, and the sons of immigrants, Jerre Mangione and Antonio Margariti.

In Chapter Four she explores the language created by Eduardo Migliaccio for his theater sketches that were popular in the early years of Italian immigration. Farfariello, as he was known, used language to bring humor, and as a by-product, criticism into the Italian immigrant experience by playing on words, regional attitudes and everyday situations.

Chapter Five examines the Identity Politics of Language through a close look at local and international efforts to maintain and promote the language with the idea of creating Italian identities in New York City between 1920 and 1940. Those looking to support the current struggle to save the College Board's Advanced Placement examination in Italian would do well to know this history.

The final chapter uses three case studies (the U.S. government through the F.B.I. Office of Strategic Service) and popular culture through the music of Louis Prima and radio programs) to show how Italian was avoided, embraced, and employed as a service to the country during the turbulent period when the U.S. was at war with Italy. An epilogue neatly summarizes the scholar's journey and marks territory for future exploration and use of this important work.

Robert Casillo
Gangster Priest (Toronto: University of Toronto Press)
ISBN: 978-0-8020-9403-2
May 2008

When I was a kid, there was no one who could turn heads faster in a funeral parlor than a gangster or a priest. So when Robert Casillo titled his new book on the Italian American cinema of Martin Scorsese *Gangster Priest*, I knew this was going to be a must read page turner. And it is.

In this close to 600 page study, with 16 pages of black and white photos and movie stills, Casillo, a gifted critic and professor of English at the University of Miami, gives thorough readings of Scorsese's "Italian American" films", and this he does better than anyone ever has, or probably ever will. He feels that these films "represent the core of his achievement" as one of American's greatest film directors. He claims that these films compare unevenly with his non-Italian American films, and he supports that claim quite well. His incredibly thorough presentation of the historical and social contexts surrounding the films and the filmmaker himself help us to see the Italian American films of Martin Scorsese in new and exciting ways.

There has been much criticism on Scorsese's films and Casillo has read it all. He has identified the limitations of previous scholarship and adroitly addressed the shortcomings of that work. His scholarship is exceptionally sound and most of all thorough, almost to a fault. Is there a source that Casillo isn't familiar with concerning Scorsese's work, Italian American culture, Catholic culture? Most prior studies of Scorsese had depended primarily on opinion-based interpretation; this one, while certainly opinionated, is composed of the most well informed opinions I have ever seen on the subject. Casillo brings an incredible wealth of knowledge to bear on the subject and takes Scorsese's films to places they have never been before in criticism.

The book's chronological structure enables the cultural, historical and biographical research for each chapter to support and enhance each subsequent chapter. At first I thought that the historical background was going to be a rehash of what has come earlier in any number of books. This never happens. And while these contexts are available in any number of other publications, rarely has it been done better or more clearly than Casillo does it here. He provides a lengthy, but worthy basis for reading Scorsese as none has before. He is incredibly thorough in his presentation and sound in his criticism. His discussion of Italian American masculinity is magnificent, and this is coming from someone who recently wrote the only encyclopedia article on Italian American masculinity. I wish I would have known Casillo was doing this work; I would have suggested that he do that article in my stead.

One of the things that Casillo does so well is to provide the reader with a socio-historical discussion of the subjects that are presented in Scorsese's films, most obviously the Mafia, but also the history of Italian American immigration and the role that Italian Catholicism played in the American Catholic church, and the result of Mediterranean versions of masculinity as the collide with their American counterparts. All in all, there is an incredible amount of scholarship here and all of it, done amazingly well.

While serving well the academic market, *Gangster Priest* is quite accessible to non-academic markets. Casillo's writing is quite smooth and clear. This is something that's changed from some of his earlier work and I'm happy to see that he's not as opaque as he used to be. This book reflects a great ability to synthesize a great deal of scholarly work and to use it to help us see Scorsese in a new light. The footnotes might seem daunting to the non-academic, but they do not have to be accessed in order to follow Casillo's argument. Those familiar with Scorsese's films will no doubt learn a great deal; those unfamiliar will learn from a truly exceptional source.

The Empire of Stereotypes (New York: Palgrave Macmillan)
ISBN: 978-1-4039-7239-2
October 2007

    Robert Casillo's latest book is priced far beyond the means of the average student who would most benefit from its contents, so this review is pitched to those of you who have money. You know who you are. You give generous cash donations in the neighborhood of a C-note or more for confirmations and graduations; you donate money for scholarships and church fundraisers, and you believe in Italian American culture. I'm suggesting that in that same spirit of the personal gift you purchase *The Empire of Stereotypes* for your family or local public library.

    Casillo is a scholar's scholar. If there is a book he hasn't read on any subject about which he writes, it's because it's not written—over one hundred pages of endnotes attest to the thoroughness with which he approaches his task. You get the impression that no page was left unturned before Casillo took pen in hand, making this study an exhausting and rewarding read. In a dizzying array of readings presented on Italian characteristics that have appeared over the centuries, he helps us understand, better than anyone before, just how and why Italian stereotypes came to be and came to cloud every public surfacing of an Italian in world culture.

Casillo painstakingly traces images of laziness, cowardice, philandering, "cicibeismo" (a bachelor's approved social attention to a married woman), found in British, German, French and American literatures and connects them to possible sources, many of which seem to flow through the writings of Germaine de Staël, the 18th century French intellectual whose criticism of Napoleon forced her into a travelling exile and eventual relocation to Switzerland. de Staël produced two very influential books: a study of European writing entitled "On Literature and its Relation to Social Institutions" and a novel, "Corinne, or Italy." Using these two books as the locus for his study, Casillo embarks on the most exhaustive exploration of just what it is that has caused certain stereotypes to be associated with people and things Italian.

Often touted as the source for Romantic notions of Italy, de Staël, as Casillo points out in his first chapter, is not so much an originator as a medium through which earlier notions have been disseminated. de Staël's power lies in how she applies her interpretation of Italian history to explain the state of Italy during her time. She blames political subjection to voluptuousness, "a trait that they inherited from their 'enervated' late Roman ancestors, this also leads to men becoming slaves to the women."

Chapters focus on the roles that a sense of balance in male/female relationships, Catholicism, Carnevale and malaria play in the way Italians are perceived. He also explores how the lack of a national government and widespread corruption in what government there was has lead to the perception that Italians are not "serious" citizens.

Throughout it all Casillo parades an impressive number of examples, seemingly incessant, for each point he makes in his compelling arguments. He illuminates the shadowy land of stereotypes as none before, creating a fountain of truth about the sources of contemporary stereotypical images that have plagued Italians who have dared to assert themselves in public arenas.

What is lacking here is a concentrated conclusion that would return to the thesis of stereotypes and synthesize the points made earlier in the work. Nevertheless, Casillo's effort helps us to see, clearly and often for the first time, various sources for the usual stereotypes, and helps us to understand their impact on subsequent representations of Italians throughout the world.

Christopher Castellani
All This Talk of Love (New York/Chapel Hill, NC: Algonquin Books)
ISBN: 978-1-61620-170-8
November 2013

Christopher Castellani has stuck closer to the streets in his work and in his art than most graduates of MFA programs. The director of Grub Street, a Boston creative writing program outside of academia, Castellani practices what he teaches and he's good at both. His latest novel builds on his earlier novels (*A Kiss from Maddelana* and *The Saint of Lost Things*), bringing some of his earlier protagonists to the brink of their mortality and others into the prime of their lives.

His focus here is the Grasso family, composed of Antonio and Maddelana, immigrants from Santa Cecilia, a mountain town outside of Rome and their children, Prima, the late Tony, and Frankie. Antonio makes his living at the Al di La restaurant, which he hopes will stay in the family when he dies. He was grooming his first son, Tony, for the job, but Tony takes things into his own hands, disappointing his father, the only one who knows the real reason why Tony opts out. The loss of Tony affects each of the Grassos differently, but all of them with the same intensity. The choices they make in their lives are all tied to the trauma of losing Tony.

Prima, a wild girl in her teens becomes a responsible housewife, raising three sons with a successful 'merican husband, becomes a mother obsessed with her boys and with the idea of taking her parents back to Italy one more time before they die. Frankie, a graduate student in English, is away at school, but finds any excuse he can to come back home to his family, the only place where he feels connected to the world. A true mama's boy, Frankie doesn't have what it takes to run the restaurant, and does what he can to avoid dealing with the loss of his older brother. Antonio can't do anything but run the restaurant until Maddalena starts needing him more and more at home. Maddalena drowns her grief in dance classes and daily phone calls with Frankie, and does all that she can to separate herself from her Italian past.

When Prima surprises them all with tickets to return to Italy, Antonio is ecstatic, Maria is adamantly against it, and Frankie sides with her. The tension around this proposed trip drives each of the Grassos into different ways of coping with the others. And in this tension, the novel moves in interesting directions.

Castellani is a master at telling each character's story without depending on one more than the other. In this way, we get a rich account of the dynamics at work in this Italian family that takes them through practical and dysfunctional behaviors. In this way, the author captures family love like no other. The novel becomes a beautiful way of seeing the real world, certainly more challenging and revealing than anything that reality television has served up. Castellani takes us all for a spin around the emotional block that encircles the relationships our family creates both within and outside our homes.

As Maddalena ages, she begins to lose track of things, and Antonio takes it upon himself to protect her from a diagnosis of oncoming dementia. Just when you think Prima's plan is lost, something happens to reverse Maddalena's feelings and the family heads off on a trip back to the Old Country, but it becomes something that none of them had imagined.

More than completing a trilogy, *All This Talk of Love*, caps character development at its best. Through simple language, even when dealing with Frankie's experience in graduate school, Castellani weaves a complex net of actions that takes the immigrant saga well beyond timeworn plots, showing us all that becoming American effects, but doesn't erase, our being Italian.

The Saint of Lost Things (New York/Chapel Hill, NC)
ISBN: 1-56512-433-2
October 2006

In *The Saint of Lost Things*, Christopher Castellani lifts two characters from his first novel, *A Kiss from Maddelena*, which won a Massachusetts Book Award, to present a new look at post-World War II Italian immigration to the United States.

Maddelena's passivity and her husband's restlessness is the recipe for a relationship meltdown, but, while theirs, at times, borders on the pathetic, it does remind us that opposites don't just attract, they sometimes can't separate. In spite of their problems with creating a family and stabilizing their place in the U.S., Antonio and Maddelena settle down only after they find ways of seeing beyond their own personal needs and dreams.

Antonio has a brother, Mario, and a friend, Renato who own a popular restaurant together. Antonio would have liked to join them in the venture, but he is afraid of letting go of the money he's managed to save from working steadily at the Ford plant. Still, he feels left out, and that his life of working in the plant and hanging out at their restaurant into the late night, is going nowhere, especially since he and Maddelena can't seem to conceive a child.

Giulio, a middle-aged mamma's boy who's lost both his parents, tries to change his name, and launch a career as a singer. He does well at the restaurant until one Christmas Eve, when he plays the accordion at the Grasso's Christmas party. After an embarrassing moment there he refuses to perform in public again. This moment endears him to Maddelena and the two find comfort in a friendship that has more to do with her inability to do anything but mother this loser, who sits at home, reading the papers, wishing his parents were still alive, always afraid of taking charge of his life. Until Maddelena and Antonio befriend him, Giulio believes, "The world turns on cruelty.... Not love. Not generosity. There are only two kinds of people left on earth—those whom grief has touched, and those it is coming for."

Castellani dramatically recreates Wilmington, Delaware's Little Italy of the 1950s with description like: "He loves the smell of bread from Lamberti's' the read, white, and green flags that hang in the storefront windows. At sunrise, not long from now, the old men will set their folding chairs on the street corners and spend the morning arguing politics in their campani dialects."

The action takes place mostly over the course of one year, but flashes back to trips to the old country. Antonio had been in the U.S. since 1936 and later returned to his home village to find a wife. He fell for one of the village's beauties, Maddelena, but his jealously often gets the better of him. When she finally gets pregnant he can only assume it's someone else's, like maybe her boss' child. The couple survives and Maddelena, in looking into the future, wishes for her children "fearlessness in all things: in love, yes, but also in work, in expectation, in the leap from the high rocks, in looking back, and in forgetting."

Castellani's new twist on the Italian immigrant story goes to tell you it's not the subject that's tiring but the style in which its presented that can make for a new story out of old material, and this novel does that better than most.

Mike Cavallaro
Parade (with fireworks) (Berkeley, CA: Image Comics)
ISBN: 978-1-58240-995-5
June 2010

They're not just for kids anymore, those things we used to call comics have made their way into what is now being called graphic literature, and with references like that they have no trouble walking in the front door of academia. But long before they could get scholarly attention, literary comics made their ways across the web and into the minds and hearts of thousands of readers young and old.

Shadowline/Image Comics got wind of Act-i-vate's web artist Mike Cavallaro's family based webcomic *Parade (with fireworks)* and they brought it into print as a graphic novel in a beautiful paperback edition. The publication was nominated for the industry's top recognition, a 2008 Eisner Award for "Best Limited Series."

The novel tells the story of Italians caught in the struggle between socialism and fascism in 1923 Italy as Mussolini's Blackshirts begin to assert (and insert) themselves into all levels of Italian society and culture. A young Paolo is introduced who comes from the country where his family runs an olive farm and exports oil to the United States. After military service in World War I, Paolo is sent to the U.S. to tend to family business in New York and Chicago, and the violence he experiences sends him running back to an Italy that has changed. When he and his friends happen upon a parade that is terrorized by thugs, Paolo defends himself and in the process ends up in justice system into which Fascism has entered. Justice is delayed, but not soon enough for Paolo and his family. The resulting tale combines history and story to create a strong sense of the injustices faced by Italians during Fascism.

Not the usual fare for cartoons, comics or even traditional fiction, Cavallaro's story, enhanced from family tellings (much to some family members dismay as the author notes in his "acknowledgements"), is a part of history that rarely sees the light of print, let alone the luminescence of comic art. Cavallaro's images are strong and stable, and his words keep the story moving and the reader wondering sometimes "did that really happen"?

Cavallaro knows when to pull the punches with language and let the images carry the story. There's a great tension between the images and the narrative, and with the fine detail that he includes in even the broadest scenes, the artist makes it possible to get by without any of the words, as though the book was the storyboard for a silent movie. The image sequence reminded me of the edgy shots and quirky editing that came upon the scene through the television series "Hill Street Blues" and "NYPD: Blue" challenging understanding through perspective and content. Sometimes the explanation for action is in the words, sometimes in the images, and all this makes the kind of story you want to read over and over again.

Mike Cavallaro was born in New Jersey and now lives in Brooklyn. He spent a couple of years at the Joe Kubert School of Cartoon Art before he began working as a freelance comic creator, illustrator and animator. Biggies like DC, Marvel, Valiant, Cartoon Network and MTV Animation are among his clients. He is working on a new web comic entitled LOVIATHAN, serialized on the web comics site, act-i-vate.com.

Paola Corso
Catina's Haircut (Brooklyn, NY: Terrace Books)
ISBN: 978-0-299-24840-6
June 2011

In *Catina's Haircut*, award-winning fiction writer Paola Corso creates a saga of immigration to the United States out of seven stories, five of which were previously published independently in journals such as *Long Story, VIA: Voices in Italian Americana, Forkroads*, and in the anthologies *The Best Travel Stories of 2006*, and *30 Days in Italy*.

While she used materials from her own family, some of what portrays also comes from researching newspapers, the Oral History Collection at the Heinz History Center's Italian American Collection in Pittsburgh. The result is a novel in stories that works as a whole because its parts, while quite different from each other, provide an overall narrative united by characters and the overarching theme.

The main characters of each story are all related to Antonio Del Negro, whose rise and fall are part of the first story. Using historical underpinnings, Corso builds a tale of innocence and the discovery of loss by a young man who finds himself out of work and trapped between the landowners and the rebel farm workers who have decided to spit in the face of fate and determine their own future. What happens in "The Rise and Fall of Antonio Del Negro" comes back through echoes in later stories, creating a satisfying chronology of a Italian family as it becomes Italian American.

The setting for some of the stories is Calabria, a land in which droughts can swallow men alive and in which floods chase people up trees and to America. Corso's mastery of magical realism appears in the next story, "St. Odo's Curse," as a young girl tries to help the village's suffering through a drought by seeking aid from a local strega, and when that doesn't work, to the local priest. Calabria. Later, when spring floods chase people out of their homes, the Del Negro family must find other ways of saving themselves.

The family joins relatives in Pittsburgh, Pennsylvania, a city, we learn in "Hell and High Water," that life is not that much different from Calabria when the famed three rivers cause The Great Flood of 1936. The last five stories happen in this U.S. setting, and we follow the generations as they learn English and ways of surviving in this new lad. Grandpa Giorgio carries with him the family legacy in things like his father's old hat. "Giorgio's Green Felt Hat," becomes a symbol of this grandfather's attempt to hold on to his past through a hat that his wife says "he'd wear in the shower if he could figure out a way it wouldn't get wet…. She was always trying to get him to take it off, because she said it made him look like a peasant, and yet that's why my grandfather liked it so much. Because he would never be mistaken for a 'patruni' in that hat". What happens to the hat becomes his granddaughter lesson in what happens when you try to hold on to material legacies.

Strange local residents each have special histories that are recounted in stories like "Jesus Behind Bars" and "Catrina's Haircut". Family history and folktale combine when a later generation returns to the family's land of origin in "Mirage". The famous "Fata Morgana" that was told to her mother by her grandmother, becomes the grail a young girl seeks when she visits her ancestral homeland for the first time. The novel's closing, "A story told and retold through the generations: father to daughter, grandfather to granddaughter and on to her children," echoes a similar opening and gives us a sense that this writing has captured stories from the oral tradition before they disappeared.

Whether you're first-, second-, or seventh-generation Italian American, this novel will speak to you about the reasons your family left Italy; you'll also gain insight into how they turned "miseria" into miracles, lost working-class identities, and much else of what enabled them to survive the tough transition to a new world.

Giovanna's 86 Circles (Madison, WI: University of Wisconsin Press)
ISBN: 0-299-21280-7 06
August 2006

Sometimes the only way to get what you deserve is to imagine it, and that's how many of the characters in Paola Corso's short fiction make their way through life. There's a danger when life becomes so predictable that you stop looking out of your window or in your mirror. When that happens to Corso's characters? Something wakes them up and turns them inside out. This talented writer shows us that this is more common than most of us know or notice, and many of these stories show us how to imagine other ways of being real.

There's nothing ordinary about the everyday people you find in the ten stories of Corso's collection entitled *Giovanna's 86 Circles*. You'll swear you know people like these, when you first start reading, but what makes Corso unique as a writer is that you won't recognize them once you get to the end of the story. There's a certain slant of realism that she fashions that skews the ordinary in strange ways. A young woman washing sheets in a hospital laundry can tell the future in the ones she folds. A woman's knitting unravels and stretches outside the house to wind its way through the neighborhood. A mayor leaks the date of his death to the press, and proves himself right.

"Yesterday's News" opens the collection with a woman taking her dead mother's clothing to a second hand clothing shop and is convinced by the clerk to keep one item that changes her life. "Between the Sheets" finds us in the laundry room of a hospital where one working tells another about her husband's illness. Things start getting weird when the window one of the washing machines turns red, and one of the worker's realizes she can see the future. "Unraveled," is a great example of how the repression of the real story by the imagination can create a tension that turns a story we've all heard before into something we want to hear again. The collection's title story is another example of this. A young boy and girl are navigating their way through their first kisses in an abandoned farm house when the legend of the previous tenants finds its way into their lives; there are two stories here that wind their ways through each other so that you realize that sometimes it's what's left behind that matters more than what was. One of the best is "The Drying Corner," in which a young girl finds a way to make her own space in her nonna's deteriorating fruit and vegetable store. This story reminds us that the young and old have much to teach each other.

Corso mines her Pittsburgh area past for what she needs to create fiction that records the past and shows us that paying attention to the little things in our own lives might just helps us better see below the surface of it all. This message comes through clearest in "Shelf Life," in which a woman's who's considered to be crazy teaches a young girl how to live off what others ignore, and that craziness is sometimes the ability to live safely outside the normal.

Some of the stories shine brighter than the others, and you can't help but wonder if some of them were rehearsals for the more successful, if not in subject, then in style, but most of them reward second and third readings, which for me, is the test of a good story. Brava!

Peter Covino and Carolyn Guinzio

West Pullman (New York: Bordighera Press)
ISBN: 1-884419-70-4
Cut Off the Ears of Winter (Kalamazoo, MI: New Issues Poetry and Prose of Western Michigan University)
ISBN: 1-930974-50-7
April 2007

T.S. Eliot wrote that "April is the cruelest month," but that was long before it officially became National Poetry Month. Considering celebrating this year by picking up these first books by young poets who have had their work recognized by the Bordighera Poetry Contest.

Peter Covino's "Cut Off the Ears of Winter," which earned him runner-up honors in Bordighera's 2000 contest, is a collection arranged around the private and public families from which we come and of which we forge ways of being alive. Divided into three sections, the poems move from outside the self, to inside the family, and finally toward community and the healing that comes from taking care of one's own pain before it hurt someone else. In a Dantesque way, we move from Purgatory, to Hell, to Paradise.

Better living through poetry, ought to be the theme of this book. Whether they're part of a city street scene, historical figures, or those strangers that come alive only through imagination, Covino's characters absorb pleasures and pain while we sit back, learning lessons and admiring the words through which they have come into our lives. The people of these poems linger in between what happened in the poet's life and what happened in his mind, reminding us that poems are like microscopes through which the smallest things take on larger meanings, like when a mother's grief calls for a son to "investigate the draft/ in the house". Section II is filled with what a family suffers and hurts because of its "Poverty of Language". Words might filter the abuse, but they do not cushion the impact of years of trauma played out on bodies and souls. This is not poetry for the weak of heart. Covino's a wise man whose art accomplishes long awaited vendettas. The final section lifts us out of a personal inferno and pulls us toward a community of healing. In it are poems more musically inclined like "The Medicine of Language."

Less accessible, but not less admirable, is the poetry which earned Carolyn Guinzio the 2004 Bordighera Prize. The prize produces a bilingual edition, and the Italian translations here have been masterfully rendered by noted Italian scholar Franco Nasi. Guinzio, a graduate of Columbia College of Chicago's poetry program earned an MFA in poetry from Bard College and has pulled together new and previously published poems to create an impressive collection that demands rereadings.

The poems in *West Pullman* are often puzzles that, while solvable, might never give us the satisfaction that what we take from them is what she wants us to get out of them. The beauty of the work here is that a depth of language that moves from shimmering surfaces to dark depths. It is this contrast, in every poem, that makes for a wonderful reading experience in which you will wonder, did I get it or not? The title poems seem to be portraits of the south Chicago neighborhood's seasons and people, yet they could also be interior monologues of a mind seeking solace through memory. The series "Flightless Rail" meditates the extinction of natural beauty. Interspersed are powerful occasional poems that turn airline flights and insect lives into moments of wonder. The collection ends with "Elsie Lamb" and reminds us that poetry is a way of seeing the world, and a good poet can make us see in new ways that which we've looked at all our lives.

Antonio D'Alfonso
Gambling with Failure (Ontario: ExileEditions)
ISBN: 1-55096-656-1
February 2009

Antonio D'Alfonso is a writer, publisher, composer and filmmaker who has spent his entire life pursuing world truth through art. Over his more than 30 years experience he has encountered many highs and lows that he records in his latest book of interviews and essays entitled "Gambling with Failure."

For D'Alfonso the journey has been a road to failure, out of which he learned to fashion whatever success he could find. The thinking reflected in his essays comes out of his realization that what society considers success is not a true measure of what should be considered successful. Bestsellers may please the market makers, but rarely do they impact a society toward any significant improvement; they are mere lullabies to the sleeping giant we call the status quo.

Born in Montreal to immigrant parents from Molise Italy, D'Alfonso was raised in the French language in schools, spoke Molisano dialect at home, and learned English to survive beyond the borders of his birthplace. This multilingual upbringing had great effects on his voice, which he modestly says is muddled by these competing cultures. He has written in French, Italian and English, and what emerges in his writing is a very interesting collage of ideas that accurately maps the effects that cosmopolitanism has on the individual voice.

Long a champion of others writings, evidenced by his creation of the press, Guernica Editions, now headquartered in Toronto, D'Alfonso has authored books of poetry, fiction, and cultural criticism. This book collects much of his work as a public intellectual. Through Op-Ed pieces, interviews of him done by others, journal entries, and a wide range of reviews and essays, he presents a strong case for the need for dissonant voices in the larger cultural community so that we can see the world for what it is, and not what established systems try to make it to be.

Some of the more interesting insights he provides come in his essays that examine Italian culture and its place in Italy and the world. He calls for creating a new understanding that would create an "Italic culture," because "Italian culture can no longer be confined to Italy." Through the study of uses of the Italian language, dialects, and culture created by Italian immigrants in other languages, we can gain a better sense of the Italian Diaspora and its impact in the world of yesterday, today and tomorrow. Only in this way can we create new ways of seeing and being that transcend the ideas of the past that trap us in a repetitive pattern of nostalgia that creates the illusion of something that no longer exists.

A weakness of the volume comes from the repetition of ideas that sometimes wallows in complaint. In spite of this flaw, one that naturally occurs when a writer collects his expressions from a wide variety of sources over a long period of time, "Gambling with Failure" presents ideas that must be reckoned with if we are to make ethnic culture matter in a time of globalization and denationalization. His notions of cultural centers, versus a single cultural center, and exporting national culture without importing other cultures, are well thought out and articulated.

D'Alfonso calls for "ethnic collectivities" to "overcome private nostalgia and the rear-view vision of culture of the first generation immigrants" so "that the serious incorporation of cultures can begin." He has bet his life's work on this idea. and only the future, close readings of his essays, will tell if the gamble was worth it.

Bill Dal Cerro and David Anthony Witter
Bebop, Swing, and Bella Musica: Jazz and the Italian American Experience (Chicago, IL: Bella Musica Publishing)
ISBN: 978-1-60461-089-5
August 2016

Long-time Chicago-area free-lance writers, often for the *Fra Noi*, Bill Dal Cerro and David Anthony Witter, joined forces to explore the incredible contributions Americans of Italian descent have made to jazz music, from its origins to today.

Written with journalistic flair, through the eyes of amateur historians, and with an the activist's bent, this compilation of profiles of major players and the overview of minor figures brings ample evidence to the great impact these composers, musicians, and singers have had on the jazz scene in U.S. history.

Short chapters composed, more often than not, in snappy style, make for quick pacing and a conversational tone throughout. There is no grand narrative arc here as each piece serves the more eclectic purpose of capturing the historical highlights from the Jazz music's birth in New Orleans's Congo Square through the interactions of African Americans Louis Armstrong and Italian Americans like Nick LaRocca—whose Original Dixieland Jazz Band recorded the first jazz record, and yet who has often been overlooked in previous jazz histories for reasons the authors explore and counter with ample treatment of his life and legacy.

Early chapters are devoted to single players like La Rocca, Louis Prima, Sam Butera, Leon Roppolo, Joe Venuti, Eddi Lang, Joe Marsala, Flip Phillips, Louie Bellson, Pete and Conte Candoli, Buddy DeFranco, Frank Sinatra, Tony Bennet, Bucky Pizzarelli, Lennie Tristano and many more. More general sections adequately introduce Jazz in Italy and Women in Jazz, and provide a breadth that earlier selections suggest.

Dal Cerro's editorializing, about the early discrimination against Italian immigrants, and the later overshadowing of stereotypes created in American journalism, appears throughout the book, often unnecessarily repeating the message that Italians had to overcome much in their efforts to assimilate into American culture. The sheer volume of Italian American presence in music alone should be enough to warrant the dispelling of stereotypes that continue to haunt the mass media presence of America's Italians, as he says, because of America's obsession with the gangster; nothing here says Italian Americans themselves have any fault in the matter for their lack of support of their own.

Beebop . . . concludes with its longest section containing cameo-like entries in what the authors call, "The Ensemble Cast," and a gathering of what might be called, outtakes in "Fascinating Facts." A bit of editing here and there would eliminate the redundancies encountered when reading cover to cover, but for those who dip in here and there, these are trivial. There are a few sections of photographs and a lengthy bibliography that point toward the rich materials from which the authors drew to create their stories.

The strongest entries are those that contain interviews conducted by the authors; the weakest, seem to be those that depend totally on research. Overall, the book earns the praise that historian Frank A. Salamone gives it in his "Foreword:" "This book is long over due. It documents the role that Italian Americans have played in the development of jazz without denying the tremendous influence made by African Americans and others."

Jazz, a truly original American contribution, might have been made by a few, but it certainly belongs to all of us, no matter our racial, ethnic, gender or class background, and Dal Cerro and Witter have provided us with an important starting point at which we can begin to appreciate its rich history.

Stephen DeFelice

He Made Them Young Again (www.authorhouse.com)
ISBN 1-4208-4178-5

One man's acida is another's well being in this what-if novel based on the author's career as a physician and world-renowned authority on medical research. Through heavily plotted scenes filled with well-ordered meals, three men try to turn back the effects of time on five elderly "doctornauts" who agree to test an anti-aging elixir. More dramatic essay than novel, *He Made Them Young Again* is low on description, but high on prescription of the doctor's philosophy of life and how to live it.

Emilio DeGrazia
Walking on Air in a Field of Greens (Minneapolis, MN: Nodin Press)
ISBN: 978-1-932472-2

Emilio DeGrazia is a prize-winning writer who somehow has managed to stay out of the limelight, avoiding fame and fortune by writing well about what matters to him, and, as it just so happens whether we know it or now, what matters to us. His latest work *Walking on Air in a Field of Greens* is a hymn (that borders on dirge) to Italian American identity.

This collection of a dozen essays works well when you read it straight through or as separate servings. There is a wonderful sense of wholeness to the collection that opens and closes with meditations on the fig tree. In between the preface and last essay lies an uncovering of a life lived in various stages of ethnic explorations.

At times, the author is proud of his heritage, at others, he can't seem to relate to its demands. All in all we get the truthful struggle of what it means to have roots in Italy and branches spreading out throughout the U.S. What is consistent throughout the collection is the fine quality of writing that takes us through each subject.

Whether it's a return trip to Italy, for the first, second or third time, of a son who's been back to San Pietro in Calabria more than his mother or father, or a visit to his retired parents' new home in Florida, the essays here are filled with expressions that we have all felt along the way to claiming or ignoring Italian American identities: "Was San Pietro my beginning point? Maybe I was at root Italian rather than American, event though I did not feel self-conscious about being 'Italian' until some of my Waspish college friends jokingly called me 'the Wop' and 'the Mafia'".

"If you want to eat, you have to work" becomes mantra that surfaces throughout the collection. It keeps the locals tied to their homes and away from the tourist sites that their visiting American relative sees and tells them about. Privileged in ways they could never be, the author often feels that his father lost out on much by leaving his ancestral land with its healthy air, peaceful surroundings, the camaraderie found when friends work together, the talking, eating and drinking with relatives long into the night, all things that the author would like to take home with him.

After his first trip back at the age of 26 he realizes that while things have changed, the past would have to remain where it was: "As the train took me father from that strange familiar land I realized that I could not carry the past across the sea. I knew now that a connection had been severed. There would be letters and memories, and always a sense that I had come from this land and these people. But I didn't think I would ever go back."

But he does return, more often through thought than travel — a few other trips throughout his life to deal with his father's land and with his own curiosity. While all the essays are strong testaments to life through thought, the one that stood out for me is "Ragionare," a powerful recollection of men working out their grief over a friend's suicide as they work scythes together across a field. "What I saw in the humor of their talk was the grief weighing down their hearts. Secretly and collectively they knew they had to let Silvio get away from them, that they had failed to anticipate what was on his him and failed to takes they small steps to prevent the suicide. Now they wondered too: if suicide was a way of getting revenge on family, was it Silvio's way of getting revenge on them?"

By the time you get to "Burying the Tree," about the rise and fall of fig trees in unnatural places, you get the sense that

DeGrazia has talked about all that matters in ethnic identity and family without ever once referring to a theory or some history larger than his own, and yet somehow has incorporated all of that stuff in his autobiographical meditations.

Rossana Del Zio
From Bread and Tomatoes to Zuppa di Pesce 'Ciambotto' (New York: Bordighera Press)
ISBN 978-1-59954-056-6
December 2012

I never review cookbooks even though I collect what I think are the best and quite often sit down to read them when I want a break from the usual fare of my career, or to inspire future meals. I have made an exception with Rossana Del Zio's *From Bread and Tomatoes to Zuppa di Pesce 'Ciambotto,'* not because I know the author, not because I have had the pleasure of tasting some of her wonderful dishes, and not because I have eaten many variations of these recipes with my family here and in our hometown of Castellana Grotte in Puglia. I am writing this review because I believe that this is a book that truly provides something unique to the culinary world—thought for food.

In his preface, John Mustaro, the President of the United Pugliese Federation of New York, tells us that he believes Del Zio has, "captured the essence of what a second-generation Pugliese longs to learn and experience, but cannot." While he doesn't go on to say exactly what that essence is or why it cannot be captured in other ways, he finds the pulse of the magic that Del Zio makes in this collection of reflections, memories, and basic recipes of Apulian culture.

Memories of the foods of her childhood include stories of she and her brother trying to cook when no one was around, of travelling merchants who, on foot, horses and carts and three-wheeled cars, sang out their presence and their products with words that waxed poetic in musical voices. But more than a memoir, this book presents a philosophic overview of the importance of eating simply and well.

From a culture of poverty came a cuisine so powerful it would command global attention as one of the healthiest, flavorful, and satisfying diets in the world. She writes that even in the poorest areas of Puglia a great deal of attention was given to the careful preparation of what went into the stomachs of one's family. The typical Apulian cuisine could bring joy to those who had given up hope that their lives would ever get better. And if their future was dark, their present could be lightened up by the foods they prepared and ate.

Cooking in Puglia was a ritual that involved the whole family. From planting, gathering, and preparing the foods that could be found within reach, fathers, mothers, children, and grandparents all had their roles. Del Zio's experiences from her own life as a participant in family meals and as a chef in various restaurants is put to good use as she presents things like the typical weekly menus of the farmers and the fishermen. For each ingredient and for every dish she give us more than a list of what to use, more than directions for preparation; she also gives us personal and communal stories of just what this food could do to the people who ate it.

This bilingual edition features such traditional dishes as Acquasale, a simple but filling cold stew of stale bread, tomatoes, olive oil and water; Chickory and Fava beans; Rice, Potatoes and Muscles; Orecchiette with Broccoli Rapa; and Panzerotti. You will also find recipes for homemade pasta, focaccia, and calzone bread, taralli, and more.

There are no exotic ingredients to track down, nor are there any complicated instructions to follow. Del Zio presents her recipes in a style of writing that entertains as it instructs. This is book you need if you long for dishes that your grandmother used to make and never got her recipes, one you'll enjoy both in the kitchen and in your favorite place to read.

George DeStefano

An Offer We Can't Refuse: The Mafia in the Mind of America (New York: Faber and Faber)
ISBN: 978-0-571-21157-9
June 2006

George DeStefano's first book is part history, journalism, commentary, and memoir on the theme of the Mafia in American culture. Neither an apologist, nor a cheerleader, DeStefano presents primarily a rehash of history already published in a variety of places, but conveniently brought together in this singularly interesting gloss. To his credit he presents previously known information in a new way to challenge the reader to think beyond Mafia when they think Italian American. For those who have made mafia mania an avocation, there's not much new except for the author's opinions and experiences. For those new to trying to understand America's infatuation with this cultural myth, DeStefano has reviewed a compelling array of sources to create an evenhanded attack on a myth and defense of a culture's good name.

Historically he's not as accurate as he could be—he misses Thomas Ince's 1915 film *The Italian* as one of the earliest film depicting Italians in the U.S., when he points to John Ford's 1924 *The Iron Horse*. To his own credit, he admits that his take on Italian American history and mafia history "are selective, interpretive, focusing on key events and issues" that come from his point-of-view as a third-generation Italian American, so we can't expect the same care of those with more academic claims. His history in the first chapter covers most of the usual sources that set up his argument that fiction has blurred the facts of Italian American culture. He follows this with a survey of the various histories and studies of Sicily's mafia and how they have been made into American images.

Chapter three begins his look at the cultural representations of the mafia in American films and television, from *Doorway to Hell* (1929) to *The Sopranos*. He interviews the likes of cultural critic Michael Parenti, novelist and fellow journalist Lorenzo Carcaterra, and scholars Richard Gambino and Robert Viscusi, to gain a wealth of other perspectives taking the study well beyond one man's view. In Chapter four, "Don Corleone Was My Grandfather," he tells of the impact this film had on his adolescence and those of countless other Italian American boys who were fashioning identities in light of the mafia mania of the 1970s. His analyses in Chapter five tend to be more like reviews than substantial criticism, the imbalance coming from more summary than critical insights being shared. While he passes over most of the more famous, and infamous, resurrections of the mafia in U.S. media, he spends most of his time on the most recent incarnation through David Chase's *The Sopranos*.

His strongest section, and most original is Chapter six, "Act Like a Man," in which he explores the mafia's relationship to changing notions of gender and varieties of sexuality. He is his best on homosexuality, and later in his critique of the Italian American *prominenti* who have used mafia representations as soapboxes to share personal opinions with the masses. The chapter on the role race play in mafia stories loses sight of the focus, but just when you thought you were out, he pulls you back in with an excellent and stirring finale with "Cultural Holocaust or National Myth?", which his is most original and controversial contribution. Here DeStefano pulls off his gentleman's gloves and gets down and dirty in his critique of NIAF's Ken Ciongoli and other key leaders of the Italian

American community. This book is a good starting place if you want learn about what the real and mythic Mafia has done to make Italian America crow, cringe, or cry out loud.

Lawrence W. DiStasi
Esty (Bolinas, CA: Sanniti Publications)
ISBN: 978-0-9652714-2-4
October 2013

What if your mother handed you a novel she had written before she died and you read it, only to realize it wasn't publishable? Most people would have set it aside with her effects, leaving it for future generations to peruse. Not Lawrence DiStasi. As he read his mother's fiction he began to respond to it with questions, comments, clarifications, compassion, outrage and joy.

In a brilliant and original move, Lawrence decided to publish his mother's novel along with his reactions to the stories. The result is a bold and innovative work entitled *Esty*, the gathering of family voices, first envisioned by Margaret Weisz DiStasi, the daughter of Esty, a Hungarian Jew. Despite, or perhaps in spite of, an arranged marriage, Esty manages to consume an affair with Vonny, her first, and it seems, only love, while her husband escapes to the U.S. to avoid World War I, resulting in Margaret's birth. But is this fact or fantasy?

This is only one of the questions that Lawrence tries to answer as he moves through his mother's story. Along the way he brings us other perspectives that he came upon as he researched some of the information in the novel. At times, Margaret stays with the fiction, at other, she strays into the reality of using real names and shifting the persons of pronouns, always maintaining that whatever anyone thinks, this is her story, and she's sticking with it.

Margaret is long dead by the time Lawrence realizes the idea of this book, but he resurrects her now and then to respond to what he has written in her — now their — book. This is where the excitement of this work intensifies, as mother scolds son for the liberties he takes, and son let's the mother know that he isn't always on her side. This interaction, along with the voices of other key figures, such as Margaret's abusive father (maybe the "not-father") marks the brilliance of Lawrence's work.

Like Esty, Margaret is forced into a marriage. Margaret is able to escape with the Italian man of her dreams who takes her from an abusive father and defends her from his attempts to make her return to her Jewish husband. Margaret converts to Catholicism and raises her family out of the shadows of her past. The excitement returns when those shadows are recast later in her life, and she must explain them to her children.

Lawrence keeps the voices separate by leaving his mother's writing in conventional format of capital letters at the beginning of sentences, while his input comes in lower-case letters.

> "the question we keep wanting to iterate is: what?
> what was the irreducible and unadorned fact that leads to this story? or that this story leads to?
> because it's the story here, that keeps us boxing with shadows. she has written a fiction and asked us to accept it as fact. or, she has written her life truth and asked us to accept it as a fiction. and the one keeps feeding and fading into the other, endlessly."

Her imagined voice returns after her death in italicized sentences: *"no, but couldn't I at least have got a son to help me with instead of—my god, don't you see what you're doing? hasn't my life been misery enough, and writing it more of a misery, isn't that enough without you making it worse? isn't it? would it be so hard to just let it be?"*

The result is one powerful and engaging read that makes us rethink our own family histories and their relationships to the socio-cultural factors that have shaped not just our present, but the very way we look at the past.

Mal Occhio (Bolinas, CA: Sanniti)
ISBN: 978-0-9652714-1-7
January 2010

It took 27 years for Lawrence Di Stasi's classic study of the evil eye to make it into paperback. During that time the author was busy teaching, researching and writing such books as *The Big Book of Italian American Culture* and editing *Una Storia Segreta: The Secret History of Italian American Evacuation and Internment during World War II*. Di Stasi's been a major force behind the American Italian Historical Association's Western Regional Chapter and has served as a board member of the Before Columbus Foundation. Recently he created Sanniti Publications and through it has reprinted *Mal Occhio: The Underside of Vision*.

This study has been a staple in my suggested reading list for years ever since I first picked it up in the early 1980s. At that time I wasn't reviewing books, but I've read it so much I had the feeling that I must have written a review somewhere. This feeling most likely came from the number of my students who have written about the subject, using (and sometimes misusing) his wonderful work. It's been a while since I last read the book so I decided to take a good look at this reprint.

Mal Occhio holds up and should be considered a classic in Italian American studies, first, because it was an original work unaided by anything else in our culture, and second, because it reads as well today as ever. The true test will be how the book will be received decades from now, and if my rereading is any indication, it will certainly resonate in our culture for years to come.

Beginning with his own family encounters of "malocchio" and the consequences of overlooking, he moves through various histories of the phenomenon in other cultures and applies what he has researched to theories about human behavior. There's more to it than mere superstition, and DiStasi tracks that all down and presents his findings in strong, logical prose. He connects his evidence to theories of psychology and theology through ideas of envy and power and finds that "The evil-eye system can thus be considered a cultural defense mechanism for handling the 'return of the repressed'".

This is the material that I must have been too young to understand fully when I first read it. It reads differently to me today, verifying the idea that there is value and beauty in taking the time to reread certain books. The experience is only one of recollection of the familiar, but reconnection to the forgotten. The familiar for me was his personal anecdotes, and the forgotten was his masterful anthropological readings of the evolution of power shift from matriarchal- to patriarchal-centered societies. His mapping of the shift in generative power, from the female creative based on the womb, to the male destructive based on the head and eye is essential for understanding contemporary power struggles.

The core lesson to be learned is that we suffer when we separate from our community and need to find ways to reconnect. He writes: "The eye, then, the eye that has gone bad, represents a fundamental anxiety in humankind. It is the anxiety over separation, in the first instance, from the protection of the mother; in every instance thereafter, from situations reminiscent of that first terrible anxiety, which is the fear of death".

A thoughtful "Afterword" is added through which he looks back on what he had written and connects it to his contemporary thinking. This reprint should find a larger audience of first readers, and for those of you who have, it's like having an old friend come back to stay in your life.

John Domini
A Tomb on the Periphery (Arlington, VA: Gival Press)
ISBN: 978-1-928589-40-2
November 2009

A young Napolitano "settebello", who dabbles in the black market, meets a beautiful and mysterious American woman. In an effort to woo her—and to show off his Neapolitan street smarts—he helps her sneak into an archeological dig and rob a tomb of its jewelry. What should have been a simple braggadocio's theft soon brings in the police, *Cammoristi*, illegal aliens, NATO officials, ghosts and more in John Domini's new novel.

A Tomb on the Periphery, the second installment in Domini's Naples trilogy, rolls history and mystery into one powerful story. Set in the same location as the first, *Earthquake I.D.*, *A Tomb* spends more time in the neighborhoods controlled by the Camorra, populated by the *clandestini*, and damaged by the earthquake more than any other area. It is in these dark quarters that the light of hope shines for Fabrizio, whose skills as a jeweler learned through his father—until the family business goes bust—are honed by the black market's need for forgeries of ancient treasures that sometimes find their way out of Paestum's archaeological digs.

With just enough university education to set himself off from his peers, Fabrizio shores up his street smarts with book smarts to arrange unique ways of supporting his ailing mother and Internet-worm brother after his father dies. He wants to avoid repeating the failures of his father's life, and that means in a country that can't employ its educated youth he must endure his mother's prayer-filled complaints and his brother's criticism.

The novel's femme-fatal, Shanti—or is it Daphne, she's pretty mysterious—works for NATO by day, but its her dark New York connections to collectors looking for archaeological bits and pieces that can be sold to collectors that draws Fabrizio into a web of action that threatens his life, shakes his core values, and rattles his usually solid sense of certainty.

Domini has created a thoroughly engaging story that stays true to its characters in voice and action. Cultural exchanges are never cursory or condescending. His creation of the world of African immigrants is vivid and sincere. Whether it's the repartee of a pair of street thugs, the wise advice of a professor, or the cat and mouse verbal and physical play of two young lovers, Domini gets it and gets it right. He renders real highly imaginative scenarios that keep mental wheels spinning and pages turning. His knowledge of what is needed to make, take and fake archaeological finds is impressive, as is his ability to keep characters real and the plot moving without a slip.

The novel's diction, often interspersed with Italian words and phrases—many effectively left untranslated—is rich, as in this description of Fabrizio's thinking as he works on a forgery after witnessing a murder: "Yet these smidgens of clarity, icy touches, bobbed for no more than a moment on the surface tension between the 'falso' under his hands and the 'terribilitia' he'd just witnessed."

The author has a keen sense of what happens where and how to make it all matters to even the most distanced of readers, as when he reveals "the real power around Naples and its periphery: the way so much unstable living could be jammed into the cavities of a single long moment, past and present and future all bursting through the seams of the same moment, so that a single mistaken step would leave you out of time, down some clotted and inescapable hole. One bad move could make you history."

Cleverly concocted and excitingly realized, "A Tomb on the Periphery" is a fine tale told by a master signifying the power behind that famous saying, "Vedi Napoli, e mori": See Naples and die!

Earthquake I.D. (Pasasdena, CA: Red Hen Press)
ISBN: 978-1-59709-076-6
October 2008

If you don't yet know John Domini, author of a couple of good collections of stories (*Bedlam* and *Highway Trade*) and a novel (*Talking Heads: 77*), then meet him through his new novel. Nominated for a Pulitzer Prize, *Earthquake I.D.*, is the first in the author's proposed Naples sequence.

In it he spins a well-focused plot tightly wound around Barbara Cantasola Lulucita, a wife and mother who discovers that her family's trip to Italy is not what she thought it would be. The surprises and mysteries cause her to doubt everything she holds dear, and pushes her into places she's never been physically and spiritually. The connection between Italian American and Italian has never been more obvious and tenuous in the same character. Barbara is on the verge of losing everything she ever wanted and in many ways has never been happier.

Jay Lulucita is a CEO who leaves his U.S. job to head up NATO sponsored earthquake relief efforts in Naples. When he gets his head bashed in during what seems to be a routine tourist mugging, his son performs the first of what will be called miracles, and Barbara's Christian faith rises as quickly as her faith in her marriage falls. With all of their documents stolen, the family become paperless like many of the "terreomotati" (earthquake victims), except under heavy security they can move through the city and the camps that temporarily shelter the tens of thousands left homeless.

Part mid-life crisis story, "Earthquake I.D." contains enough of a mystery to keep the pages turning, and it is one contemporary story that can touch us all. There's no nostalgia in the way Barbara and Jay look back on their lives. When these ugly Americans find themselves hostage beneath the ruins, they come to learn more about each other than they have in the nearly 20 years of their marriage. And the same seems to be happening to their children: a precocious teenager who falls in love with a gypsy girl, a prepubescent boy who performs miracles that save lives and gets international attention, and twin girls who could have easily been conjoined as they move and speak identically. Barbara's mother-in-law visits. She can be left alone with children, but not the priest who is confessor of both Barbara and Jay.

When Cesare the priest crosses the line he ends up confessing his own sins out loud to whomever will listen. The actions and antics of the entire group will help you step beyond the reality that Domini so well creates, and makes you question just what kind of world we're living in. The family faces personal problems amid national emergencies, and in the process find it's hard to realize intimacy when you're dealing with global realities. When Barbara's son is touted as a new savior, we are reminded how we are when we want people to be what we need; we often refuse to separate the person from the public personality.

The geographical and economic contrasts of Naples reflect the contrasts that Barbara learns to see inside her self and the "normal" life that she had been living so simply and uncontemplated until this trip. Naples, above and underground is rendered in exciting detail, and casts some interesting light onto Italy's immigration issues, especially the "clandestini". There's no doubt that Domini's story will raise interest in his related works which are due out soon, so keep an eye out for the next installment, *A Tomb on the Periphery*.

David Evanier

The Good Life (New York: John Wiley and Sons, Inc.)
ISBN: 978-0-470-52065-9
May 2012

Tony Bennett has long been the subject of entertainment critics, journalists and historians, so you'd think by now we've heard it all. He's even told his own story in the *The Good Life* in 1998, and yet, in spite of all the ink that's been spilled on his life, something different happens in the hands of seasoned biographer David Evanier. The former editor of the Paris Review is a top fiction writer and author of biographies of Jimmy Roselli and Bobby Darin. His "All the Things You Are: The Life of Tony Bennett" is a careful composition of the making of an artist and the personal and public obstacles he overcame to achieve iconic status in American popular culture. Evanier covers the shadows as well as the spotlights of Bennett's life to paint a fuller portrait of the singer and the man than we've ever seen.

Not many know that during World War Two Bennett witnessed the horror of a German concentration camp when his unit liberated a Bavarian concentration camp in Landsberg, or that he once entered an army mess hall with a black friend who was denied entry—an act for which Bennett was demoted on the spot when a sergeant cut off his corporal stripes. These early experiences shaped Bennett's social conscience, leading to his anti-war stance and his support of the Civil Rights Movement in the 1960s.

Born Anthony Benedetto in 1926 in Queens, New York to children of Calabrian immigrants, Tony Bennett sees his poor upbringing as a plus in his career, something that has given him a solid foundation not just for his life, but for his career as one of America's top crooners. Starting out as a singing waiter with the stage name Joe Bari, Bennett appeared on *Talent Scouts*, a precursor of contemporary shows such as American Idol, where he came in second to Rosemary Clooney. From there he went on to a career that included traveling to Italy with Count Basie where he was booed and "barely got out of the town alive."

Evanier utilizes many of the previous accounts and interviews that have appeared in books, newspapers, and magazines throughout Bennett's long career. He quotes extensively from them, sometimes a bit too much, for Evanier's voice is more than adequate in getting the information across. He skillfully counters this excess through original interviews with Bennett's friends and collaborators, sources that often contradict each other to give us a more complex sense of the singer's life.

Loyal to family, friends, and fans, Bennett maintained a close relationship with Frank Sinatra, his mentor in many ways, and built a New York school for the arts in Sinatra's name. He once made a phone call to get a friend's mother into Villa Scalabrini, a suburban Chicago home for the aged, for which he, like Sinatra did benefit concerts.

What's most amazing is that Bennett continued to sell out concerts and produce classic songs throughout the rise of Rock and Roll, the British Invasion, Disco and more, without caving into pressure to follow the trends. With the help of his sons, Danny and Daegal, he has been able to connect to the MTV generation and maintain a public presence like no other musical artist. Beyond his singing, he has become a serious artist who has produced works that are exhibited and hang in museums and private collections throughout the world.

Evanier artfully captures the essence of Bennett as "a transcendent singer, . . . an entertainer, a painter, an educator, a troubadour, a messenger of hope and optimism, and a loyal and faithful servant to the regular guy on the street. He is our street singer, our true democratic spirit, our messenger of hope."

David Evanier is the author of *Making the Wiseguys Weep: The Jimmy Roselli Story*, *Roman Candle: The Life of Bobby Darin* and other works of fiction and non fiction.

Carol Faenzi
The Stonecutter's Aria (openlibrary.org: Aperto Books)
ISBN: 0-9767949-1-8
February 2007

Some people try to tell family history through stories, some family stories through history, but neither would work for corporate communications specialist Carol Faenzi, so she decided to make her family live through a prose form of opera. *The Stonecutter's Aria* is an ambitious attempt to do something new with Italian American history and personal memoir, and in some ways she succeeds in both.

Using her great grandfather's immigration to the U.S. as a starting point, Faenzi's overture takes us into Aristide's thoughts as he travels from Carrara, Italy through Ellis Island, to New York city, Barre, Vermont, Sunnyside plantation in Alabama, eventually winding up in Indianapolis. A first act follows that brings us the main characters of his nuclear family: wife, Ione, daughter Olga, son Giorgio, with a few minor neighborhood folks appearing along the way.

Act One, presents a pretty typical immigration story that gets bogged down with too much historical information from the author's research. The stories of the different characters is a great idea that never reaches its potential because there is no noticeable voice difference among the characters. We can't tell the bass male voice from that of the female soprano. What we get is the author's voice telling the stories of each character, and this tends more toward the didactic than the dramatic. The author tells us what she's learned when she should let her characters show us; this is what happens Italian Americans write without reading much of each other and try to do it all with one book. It would be enough to tell Aristide's family stories and not worry about Italian American history.

Father and son speak in an "Intermezzo," and Act Two, takes the characters through World War II and more into the lives of Olga and her husband Otto (the author's grandparents). Aristide is a master sculptor who has worked on some of the greatest American monuments made from granite and marble. With his son he worked on site of the Lincoln Memorial, Our Lady of Mt. Carmel Cemetery outside of Chicago, and much more. Once again, Faenzi is at her best when she lets the characters tell their stories, at her weakest when they are reciting historical facts. Still the voices never vary.

The author rescues the work with a strong third act in which she enters the tale as one inspired by her grandmother's gifts of "a love of Italy, of opera, a talent for cooking without a recipe… [and] the courage to travel and seek my dreams". This is where the drama picks up and we get to see behind the scenes of the earlier acts. Faenzi's experiences as a Jehovah's Witness and her trips to Italy make for the greatest drama of this work.

Faenzi honors her ancestors' lives with her words, but beyond this, she reminds us that we are made of the lives that came before us and can only be happy with what we are when we know who they were and how their lives came to affect ours. When all is sung and done, we end up with a hit and miss experiment that brings great insight into the effects one generation has on the next along with the tired historical lessons heard so many times before. This first book reads like one, but doesn't fall apart at its weakest points.

Gil Fagiani
A Blanquito in El Barrio (www.rainmountainpress.com)
ISBN: 978-0980221138
June 2011

What's a nice Italian boy like you doing in a barrio like this? Gil Fagiani answers that question and more in his latest book of poetry. *A Blanquito in El Barrio* moves chronologically through the poet's life on the streets of Harlem covering his 1960s' journey from drug abuser to drug counselor, from eye closer to eye opener. There's tough stuff here and the way its rendered and filtered through art makes it all worthwhile. Here city life at its worst and best is captured in compelling verse.

Maria Fama
Looking for Cover (New York: Bordighera Press)
ISBN: 1-884419852
January 2009

    Maria Fama is a seasoned poet who has a number of awards to her credit including the Aniello Lauri Award (twice) and the Amy Tritsch Needle Award; her poetry has also earned honorable mention (twice, and she's been a finalist for the Allen Ginsberg Poetry Award. There is nothing pretentious about her poetry. Her latest book is something to pick up for everyone interested in pure and simple play with language. Divided into four parts, *Looking for Cover* is Fama at her best.

    Part One, "Shields and Shelter," is the result of some great archaeological digging into her ancestral history, and in it we find writing around the themes of immigration history that avoids the typical nostalgia associated with dead grandparents. Fama finds a way for the past to connect to the present so that the future is fed by the wisdom of the ancients. We often joke about how often people commemorate the lives of immigrant grandparents in their poetry, and how maudlin so many of them are. But nobody works better with this material in poetry than Fama. In "Pasta and Piselli," the poet finds the pride inside the poverty her grandmother experienced. Part history, part recipe, the poem captures the life of an immigrant in a unique way. Fama achieves a striking nobility through simple storytelling here and through the creation of a "poor people's feast". All of the poems in this section preserve a family legacy that speaks through memories of immigrant ancestors.

    Part Two "Doorways and Crossroads," presents poems that deal with the process and products of American assimilation. The theme of civil rights and race comes through clearly; in "I

Am Not White", a dentist says her teeth tell of mixed blood, and through it comes the history of her people, "I am Sicilian/I am not white" she responds in a defiant take on identity. The poems here tell of identity building experiences. "Fireworks on July 4, 1004," recalls her father's experiences in World War II through the writer's take on today's war in Iraq. Some of the poems capture neighborhood life and the social realities of events like the "Valentine Teen Dance at the Aquarama".

"Spirit World," presents poems such as "August Heat" and "Summer Story 1993," that are mediations on life and nature. Through rituals and sensory imagery memories the poet conjures memories that mark the passage of time that have marked the poet's life with sacred scars.

The final section, "Under the Tent," contains a number of Fama's performance poems. A weaker one is the title poem "Looking for Cover," but there are a few that are simply breathtaking. In "Watching Dizzie Gillespie on TV," she moves from words to scat and back so that the sounds surround the meaning. This is truly performance poem that must be sung to feel its magic. There's also, "Comari" about the female friends and Marys in her life. My favorite of this section is her poem about St. Anthony, which you've got to hear to appreciate: "Antony, Antonius, Antinuous, Antonio/ all the ancients converge on your name/ all those who carry your finding found name/ are not and ever converging/ Tonio, Ant, Tony, Nino, Tonio/ Tony the Tiger, Tony Martin, Tony Taylor, Tony Bennet/

While these are all interesting on the page, they work much better when heard, and for an extra $6 you can purchase the CD through SPDbooks.org and hear the poet's own voice as she performs these wonderful works.

Jean Feraca
I Hear Voices: A Memoir of Love, Death, and the Radio (Madison, WI: the
  University of Wisconsin Press)
ISBN: 978-0-299-22390-8
August 2008

Jean Feraca is known for her ability to listen and engage in conversations that make for award-winning radio program, "Here on Earth," which she has hosted and produced through Wisconsin Public Radio for many years. The author of three books of poetry, much of which deals with her Italian ancestry and experiences as an Italian American, Feraca has recently published *I Hear Voices: A Memoir of Love, Death, and the Radio*.

The seven personal essays cover a range of subjects from her childhood to her life today. The most powerful of these essays are the first two, which focus on the lives and deaths of her brother and mother. "My Brother/The Other," is mediation on her brother Stephen's long illness and death. Stephen, a Columbia University trained anthropologist, was an expert in American Indian culture, and lived a unique life for which he never apologized. Strong, sensitive, yet stubborn, Stephen was very much the opposite of Jean in the way he approached life and relationships. Jean's account of his life is honest, and reveals as much about her own strengths and weaknesses as it does about his. He could be a saint or a sinner, depending on his mood, and Jean manages to tell his story with compassion and enough detachment to keep us caring about what happens to them both.

"Dolly: the mystery at the end," the essay on her mother, is so incredibly honest that it sometimes hurts, especially when we understand that she voices feelings that all of us have had, and few would ever admit to ourselves, let alone to others. "My mother was a monster who lived well into her nineties," is the opening line and from there this piece takes off to cover the incredible stories of her mother's real and imagined lives. Along the way, this child of the 1930s, lives a normal life as long as her husband's alive, but after his death, she lets go in strange and abnormal ways. We find ourselves cheering her rebellion and relating to her child's embarrassment at the behavior through which she refuses to "Go gentle into that good night." This account of an old woman's rage, and unique sense of public presence is both refreshing and reprehensible, and forces us to have second thoughts about striving to reach that "cent'anni" we have toasted to along the way.

The least effective essays, and perhaps most self-indulgent, are "Get Thee to a Winery" and "Why I Wore Aunt Tootsie's Nightgown," which seem to suffer more from hyper-self-consciousness than overwriting. Coming after the earlier chapters on her mother and brother, might be what does it, and makes them more like the stuff of ordinary, undistinguished memoirs. But this poet can write well about her self, as we see in the final three essays.

"Caves," is perhaps the most poetic of them all, and uses beautiful metaphors to explore the evolution of her creativity from poetic awareness and training with the master poet Donald Hall through her earliest artistic efforts, culminating with the production of award winning poetry. This is a strong statement of professional development that avoids the pitfalls of narrating one's way through a resume. The last major essay in the collection deals with a trip to the Amazon that resulted from one of her radio shows, that tests all her skills as a human being and writer. The final essay, "A Big Enough God," is a prayer-like meditation on the differences between her atheist husband and her God-fearing self and helps us to understand the beauty of a life lived with a strong self in mind that is fashioned through words.

Tom Ferraro
Feeling Italian: The Art of Ethnicity in America (New York: New York University Press)
ISBN: 9780814727478
December 2005

Feeling Italian: The Art of Ethnicity in America is Tom Ferraro's long awaited study of Italian American culture. Ferraro writes to educate and entertain, and this new book is accessible to anyone interested in early 20th century America.

In ten separate essays, Ferraro covers the range of Italian American history from the 19th through the 20th century by examining a number of cultural actors, acts and artifacts that Americans of Italian descent have contributed over the years. His thesis, throughout the book is that in becoming Americans, Italian immigrants have Italianized the United States is ways that transcend Little Italys.

He starts with the story of the infamous Maria "the murdering seamstress" Barbella, who in 1895 killed a man who had preyed upon her and garnered international attention in her trial. Ferraro analyzes both the historical record and Idanna Pucci's documentary novel "The Trials of Maria Barbella" in an effort to show that the southern Italian sense of honor provoked a crime that most Americans could only imagine. In the process she gets away "in a cultural as well as literal terms – with murder".

What follows is similarly smooth analyses of Frank Stella's paintings, Pietro di Donato's 1937 short story "Christ in Concrete", which eventually became a novel of the same name, Mario Puzo's best novel, *The Fortunate Pilgrim*, the musical mystique of Frank Sinatra, Puzo's and Coppola's *Godfathers*, *Moonstruck*, the career of pop diva Madonna, racial issues in the context of the acting career of the African-Italian American Giancarlo Esposito, and finally Stanley Tucci's *Big Night*. He concludes with a brief gloss of *The Sopranos* to show us just how Italian the United States can become. Rather than burden the reader with too many heady footnotes, he saves all his bibliographical information for a brief narrative essay that he tacks on the end to remind us that this book is the result of much reading and thinking over the years.

Through it all Ferraro shows us all that scholarship can be fun. You can tell that he enjoyed doing the research and writing and that he has developed his thinking through his teaching. His conversational style, which borders glibness, will bring in more readers than most academic tomes. He explicates the art by Americans of Italian descent by historicizing the production and reception and by applying sophisticated critical tools to move us beyond the more mundane responses given by many of the earlier critics. Beyond the scholar's job of helping us understand ideas, Ferraro fulfills the critic's responsibility of making art matter in ways we might not have previously realized. He speaks well to the relevance ethnicity has to thinking and being American.

Feeling Italian is a smart book, one that thinks and makes the reader think beyond the usual. The essays here all reflect his ability to synthesize major critical thought and apply it to his subject in unique and innovative ways. As we have seen in his earlier essays, such as "Lorenzo's Chrism," Ferraro never takes on a subject without first mastering a number of contexts through which that subject can be analyzed. Be it religion, art, music, or film, Ferraro covers each subject with the background that comes only from good research and meditative thinking about the subject. This book might not get you to think Italian American, but it should get you to feeling it, and that, says

Ferraro is more than you can hope for from a hyphenated American culture like the Italian Americans.

Valerie Fioravanti
Garbage Night at the Opera (Kansas City, MO: BkMk Press)
ISBN: 978-1-886157-84-2
August 2013

Valerie Fioravanti has been publishing stories for years in places like the *North American Review*, *Cimarron Review*, and *Hunger Mountain*. Four of hers received Pushcart Prize nominations and a Special Mention in Pushcart Prize XXVIII. Now many of them appear in the collection *Garbage Night at the Opera*, which won a G.S. Sharat Chandra Prize for Short Fiction.

Educated at the New School in New York and New Mexico State University, Fioravanti is a native of Brooklyn, New York who now lives in California where she teaches writing online at the UCLA Extension and runs the Stories on Stage program in Sacramento. Recently she was awarded a Fulbright Fellowship to work on a novel set it Italy.

What Firoavanti does better than anything else with these stories is create a world that rarely makes the media these days in any kind of positive light. Politicians talk around it; pundits pretend it doesn't exist; and those who live in it are led to believe that they are not part of it. That is the world of the working class majority—the people who make it possible for massive amounts of wealth to be amassed by an incredible few. These are the people who have been duped into accepting cutbacks in all areas of their lives. The result? They receive less than previous generations for their work, turning the dream of working one's way out of poverty into a recurring nightmare not unlike the myth of Sisyphus.

Fioravanti's characters are those who lived in the little Italys long after they became viable as ethnic islands. Hers are characters who worked the docks, the factories, the bottling plants: those who pursued higher wages rather than higher education; those who turned to drink when it hurt to think; to violence fueled by the frustration of solving problems became too much. But even in these dismal, destiny-driven lives there remains the hope that something, be it through religion, art, love, family, or friendship, will help them transcend their daily drudgery.

In the opening story, Massimo, an out-of-work father wants only for his daughter to see an opera at the Met so that she can experience the beauty that is often denied to workers who don't have the time, the energy, the money to take in the arts. When they arrive at a sold out performance without reserved tickets, they take refuge in Central Park and find treasure in what other ignore.

Most of the stories involve women and young girls as protagonists who must navigate their way through school bullies, randy neighbor boys, and men who drink their way to power. How they survive is the stuff of dramas that make for very worthwhile reading. Fioravanti is never over-literary; her prose draws attention to its subjects and not to the writer through direct, evocative description and dialogue that rings true to the streets. Whether it's a first kiss, in "Kissing Decisions," or supporting a family of the unemployed, in "Earning Money All Her Own," we witness women raised in the traditions of patriarchy, fighting to hold families together without losing their self-respect. Some win, some lose, but all of them reveal the reality of lives dependent for survival on forces outside of their own control.

Those who do succeed in getting ahead can take vacations, as in "Mayan Sunset," but when these folk leave the neighborhood, for a well-earned escape, they find the time to contemplate the "what ifs" that change the ways they look at their lives. And when these women leave their neighborhood, for school, for work, for play, they are often recognized and restrained by those who think themselves to be above the working class.

Mario G. Fumarola
The Last of the First (SPQR Company)
ISBN: 978-0692014028
December 2012

In *The Last of the First*, Mario Fumarola gives us Tony, a child of Italian immigrants, who now in his seventies knows that he might be one of the few left to give testament to the remarkably ordinary lives those immigrants fashioned as they severed ties from one country and grafted them on to another. While Tony is not his real name, as the storyteller states up front, he does participate in an accounting of life that was real for those children of Italian immigrants who grew up in the 1940s.

This is Fumarola's final book in his Utica, New York Trilogy, which began with *Wasn't it Only Yesterday*, followed by *Immigrants All*. This third book, more novel than the previous, shifts between Tony in the present—a man in his seventies who drinks more than he should and smokes a daily Toscano cigar, in the manner of the men he watched as he was growing up, and his past, as a child who saw everything with the eyes of wonder, and now, as an adult, finally begins to understand all the reality that contributed to those wonders.

Tony shifts between past and present by using "Page Up" and "Page Down" divisions as though the story was one document where past or present can be accessed at will. And of course, this is what the storyteller can do in his mind. Fumarola's characters can be found in every little Italy. There's Johnny the baker boy who in the course of making deliveries finds a customer who is willing to help him leave his boyhood. Then there's Hat Box Becky and a pint-sized man called Hammer—for reasons dramatized in one of the stories, There is Nichols Louie, the Western Union supervisor who is the first to receive the news of loss to the families of those serving in World War Two. When La Signora Partelo reads the telegram about her son she sends out a scream that ripples throughout the neighborhood, affecting man and animal alike. When the American Legion representatives visit the house, their racist attitudes get shaken as never before.

In fiction that reads like a life-story, Fumarola helps us all to know what it was like to live in those neighborhoods of difference that came together when "The Good War" came along.

We see it all, the good news and the bad, the happy times and the sad, through the eyes of an aging man whose grandchildren may never know what really goes on inside their nonno unless they read his book. And when they do they will realize that Tony was the neighborhood scribe, the one who preserved a version of all of their lives during a time when people were so busy making ends meet that rarely had the chance to see it all make sense as it does in Fumarola's stories. This verbal scrapbook of yesterday tells the stories of those who couldn't tell their own, capturing the end of one generation as it leaves life to the next.

One of the strongest stories belongs to Joey, a soldier in the Korean War, who is taken as a prisoner of war and who dies of starvation in the camp. The materials for this story come from something Tony calls, the Melchiorre file, a gathering of letters, documents, and newspaper articles about the events taking place in and around the Melchiorre house. The author uses actual hand written letters and a telegram to anchor the reality of this tragedy in the lives of those who suffered more as they had to live with the memory of such events. Accompanying the stories are the illustrations Charles Favreault that accent the stories.

Gerald R. Gems
Sport and the Shaping of Italian American Identity (Syracuse, NY: Syracuse University Press)
ISBN-9:780815633419.
July 2014

Quite often we take our sports heroes to be individuals, at best, symbolically connected to the racial and ethnic groups they come from. But in Gerald R. Gems' new study, "Sport and the Shaping of Italian American Identity," the impact of ethnic culture helps us to see just what helped to produce thousands of sports heroes from the Italian American Community. From Joe DiMaggio to Joe Montana, Donna Caponi to Marylou Retton, the efforts of Italian immigrants and their descendants have shaped the history of American sport. If a casual glance at sports history in the United States provides a wealth of positive representation of Americans of Italian descent, just imagine what an in-depth study can do.

Gems, a professor of Health and Physical Education North Central College in Naperville, IL, digs deep into American sociological and cultural history to help us understand the role that ethnicity plays in the development of an individual's success in sports. Through thorough readings of the many studies that preceded his, Gems gleans pertinent information that provides rich insights into the Italian American presence in American sports — something he sees both as ways of maintaining ethnic identity and enabling it to change as immigrants move from Italians to Americans.

Beginning with what he sees as a lack of national identity, due to the timing of mass emigration from Italy, Gems builds a strong case for explaining how Italians, through participation and excellence in American sports, fashioned new American identities while preserving older, useful aspects of Italianitá. This is the key to understanding the evolution of Italian America. Gems uses many sources from a variety of scholarly disciplines to present first, a cultural study of Italian immigration to the United States, and then a sociological explanation of the movement of working class Italians from urban and rural centers of initial settlement to the suburban middle class. His work on race tackles the difficult questions of the role whiteness plays in shaping American identities.

There are no pictures, as one would expect in a book that deals with some of America's most iconic figures. Everything is presented in words that explain the various ways that sports shaped Italian Americans and how they, in turn, reshaped America. "Italian successes not only developed an ethnic pride and a great national identity," he writes, "but head-to-head competition offered the opportunity to dispel notions of physical inferiority and gain a measure of retribution for ethnic slurs and insults that accompanied the stereotypes of Italians." Finally, we have, in one place, the source of a great deal of ethnic pride.

Gems, balances the highs and the lows of sports history by not avoiding the shame that accompanied some aspects of assimilation that often appears through reverse racism, created in part by historical amnesia and ignorance of the immigrant past. The same Italians who were discriminated against on the playing field, sometimes turned into racists themselves. Whether it was the individuals who expressed their racism as a way of belonging to the mainstream majority, or the African-American and Italian-American groups that fought over figures such as Franco Harris, the Italian American presence in sports and fanatic spectatorship has become a microcosm of what's gone right and wrong in the United States.

Taking on the world of sports as a whole, Gems' study adds depth to previous books such as Lawrence Baldassaro's *Beyond DiMaggio: Italian Americans in Baseball*, and the Wikipedia compilation of Italian Americans in boxing, and transcends Nick Manzello's biographical study *Legacy of the Gladiators: Italian Americans in Sports*, to present a rich and detailed study worthy of attention by scholars and everyday sports fans alike.

Maria Gillan

All That Lies Between Us (Toronto: Guernica Editions)
ISBN: 10-1-55071-262-6
December 2005

From her first book of poetry, *Flowers from the Tree of Night* (1980), to her most recent, *Women in Black Dresses* (2002), the family has been a regular subject in the work of Maria Mazziotti Gillan. In her latest book, *All That Lies Between Us*, the poet views the idea of family from a perspective that is quite different from her earlier works, defying centuries old proverbs that warn against revealing personal information in public.

The poet puts her personal life out there in a way that makes her incredibly vulnerable, and by doing so her poetry becomes all the more powerful. Gillan tells the truth in ways that make the reader blush, and she can do this with ease now that she has become the survivor who is now the family's matriarch. It's as if she's told the world "I have been a good girl holding back and saving face long enough; now sit back and listen to my truths."

Here are confessions of what she fears: "What a Liar I am," exposes lies she had to tell to live without harming those she loved, and "Your Voice on the Phone Wobbles" is one of the truths about life that have hurt her more than the lies. These poems become ways of confronting those things in her life than cannot be ignored, hidden away in drawers, swept under carpets, or tossed out with the trash.

Most of the poems look backward over a life filled with gain and loss, and the voids created by the losses get filled with her words and stories. Grief is no longer conquered by joy, but sits along side it in her life as if to create a balance that only the mature know: you can't have one without the other.

The losses of loved ones, a mother, a father, a sister, become occasions to recall past happiness, but unlike earlier poems, these do not celebrate the emotional highs, but seem to steep in those emotional lows that accompany depression and force us to find new ways to cope with fears and sorrows, and it is in this coping that we come to more fully understand our lives.

Yes, many of the poems are depressing, but as Gillan has reminded us in all of her past work, if life is a bowl of cherries, then eating them stains your fingers and after the pleasure and nurture they provide, you are left with the pits. Most of these poems are indeed meditations on those pits of life and death and sometimes you can't tell the difference. In true Italian fashion, she brings the dead back to live in "People Who Live Only in Photographs". "I want to write a poem to celebrate" memorializes objects and events from her past, and while nostalgia creeps in every now and then, she beats it back with strong doses of how you must be strong to face the trials of aging.

There are poems that map the ups and downs of her marriage built on images of her husband and her as life goes on. Wile is seems she might be begging for sympathy and pity — the juxtaposition of his handsome figure in youth, and his slow physical deterioration by disease is almost too much to bear — she never wallows in it for she not only recalls the good times, but the bad as well. In some other hands this might all become mawkish and pathetic, but Gillan shows us how such experiences become the foundation for a building of new strengths that can enable the acceptance ways of moving beyond such traumatic events through a focus on creating art.

Edvige Giunta and Joseph Sciorra
Biancheria: Critical and Creative Perspectives on Italian-American Women's Domestic Needlework (Jackson, MS: University Press of Mississippi) ISBN: 978-1-62846-013-1.
June 2016

This collection of writings from forty artists, poets, scholars and storytellers evolved from a 2002 conference held by the John D. Calandra Italian American Institute entitled *Biancheria: Critical and Creative Perspectives on Italian-American Women's Domestic Needlework*. The editors searched beyond the conference presentations to gather a dynamic selection of artifacts, artworks, poetry, stories personal and scholarly, and illustrations of the makers and the made.

As the editors state in their "Introduction:" "What inspired our search for representations of women's domestic needlework was the capacity of a simple object—or even the memory of that object—to become something else: literary, visual, performative, ethnographic, or critical reimagining. The process by which these transformations occur is the subject of this book."

From the editors' essay, which does much more than introduce the volume, to the touching "Afterword" by Donna Gabaccia, a scholar and practitioner of needle arts herself, there's not a weak stitch in the text. This is the kind of collection you probably won't read in the order presented, but if you do, you'll be see the art of good editing at work. Each poem, memoir, scholarly investigation and artists' statements accompanying images of their work, seems to feed from and add to what's presented earlier.

The wonderful poetry of Sandra Gilbert, Maria Mazziotti Gillan, Paola Corso, Maria Terrone, Peter Covino, Rosette Capotorto, Giuliana Mammucari, Marisa Frasca, Gianna

Patriarca, Barbara Crooker, Peter Covino, Phyllis Capello, Anne Marie Macari, Denise Calvetti Michaels, Paul Zarzyski, are scattered throughout the volume, serving as artistic *intermezzi*.

Memoirs by Louise DeSalvo, Lia Ottaviano, Joanna Clapps Herman, Tiziana Rinaldi Castro, Annie Rachele Lanzilloto, Jo Ann Cavallo, Giovanna Miceli Jeffries, are all rich with the details and attitudes that recapture the lives of those who left these lace made objects for use to use, abuse and muse over as new families are made of the old. Each writer crafts words as carefully as the subjects of their writings treated their cloth creations.

Scholarly essays by Hwei-Fen Cheah and Ilaria Vanni on Australian women's lives, Christine F. Zinni on women in upstate New York, Mary Jo Bona on needlework in Italian American literature, Jennifer Guglielmo on the relationship between needle work and labor migration, Bettina Favero on immigrant woman workers in Argentina, Joan Saverino on women from Calabria and Joseph Inguanti, all look at how, in Inguanti's words, "*bianchieria* embodies values that fostered the construction of an Italian American worldview, identity and culture." They are all strong and together give us a great sense of how the source of the Italian Diaspora touched the lives of so many immigrants and their subsequent generations.

Visually interesting are the examples of needlework by Maria Grillo (told by her daughter Lucia), and the art that incorporates objects and finished needlework. Included here are B. Amore, Lisa Venditelli, Karen Guancione, Angela Valeria, and Elisa D'Arrigo, each example adds a deep, material dimension to the writings.

In sum, you have a treasure here of wonderful writings about a subject that touches all of our lives, whether it's trough the lace doilies on the arm rests of your living room chair, the knitted coverings of clothes hangers, bed sheets or the old cedar chest that once protected the trousseau. Giunta and Sciorra have crafted a thought-provoking collection of writings that, like the subjects they treat, preserve a distinct sense of the importance and the value of work made art, and art that works to help us review the past as we carry these traditions into the future.

Jennifer Guglielmo
Living the Revolution (Chapel Hill, NC: University of North Carolina Press)
ISBN: 978-0-8078-3356-8
April 2011

One of the best-kept secrets of Italian American culture is the power that women have created and continue to wield in the Italian American family and communities throughout history. Jennifer Guglielmo, an assistant professor of History at Smith College, offers a commanding corrective to earlier images of immigrant women as weak pawns in the larger scheme of American immigrant history with her study *Living the Revolution: Italian Women's Resistance and Radicalism in New York City, 1880-1945*.

Using many of the same sources that have contributed to Italian American history, Guglielmo uncovers material overlooked and ignored by previous historians to present a strong historical reality revealing the important roles Italian immigrant women have played in resisting traditional social and political forces in Italy and the Americas. Written for students, scholars and the general reader, *Living the Revolution* is not women's history so much as it is more fully developed American history.

"Women's Cultures of Resistance in Southern Italy" opens the study and shows how migration challenged traditional social structures and forced women to fill the voids created by the men who left first in great numbers. She offers insight as to how earlier misconceptions came to be: "The now familiar tropes of Italian peasant women as submissive, ignorant victims can be traced directly to Italian bourgeois attempts to possess such insurrectionary women in order to secure their own social and economic position" (12-13). Guglielmo finds acts of power in the world of mysticism and spirituality through which women "created a counterideology, an alternative way of understanding the world that permitted their own expression, power and self-determination" (27).

The author uncovers a rich history of collective action taken by women through kinship and neighborhood connections that often led to participation in the more notice acts of revolt through the social and political movements of labor unions, cooperatives, anarchism and brigandage, proving that the "white widows" of migrant males were anything but passive in their adjustment to life without male supervision.

In "La Sartrina (The Seamstress) Becomes a Transnational Labor Migration" Guglielmo shows how young women educated by their elders took their skills and experiences working together with them when they immigrated, and drew from their experiences to create bases of power through with they supported each other as they contributed to the survival of their families. Enhancing traditional sources through a lively use of oral histories, Guglielmo draws distinctions among the ways the nations of Argentina, Brazil and New York, attempted to assimilate Italian immigrant workers and shows how women experiences of resistance to their new environments.

In "The Racialization of Southern Italian Women" she shows how immigrant women could transcend "old world" either-or roles such as "virgin-whore", and yet in the U.S., were more likely to be seen as a helpless victims of circumstances beyond their control, especially when compared to U.S. American middle class women and the Italian men. With conditions of work conflated with her identity, the immigrant woman workers were positioned as either deserving of their situation or in need of rescue. Guglielmo offers a great deal of evidence to show how immigrant woman countered such stereotypes especially because they were able to obtain the privileges of whiteness, albeit often through an inferior version than middle class white women.

Her chapter, "Surviving the Shock of Arrival and Everyday Resistance," gives light to the way that Italian immigrant women "translated daily acts of resistance and survival as they adapted to new settings." Whether it's a response to the suggestions of settlement house guidelines or a defiance of the conditioning of their children through U.S. social institutions, women were not passive acceptors of forces beyond their control; such acts served as foundations for new ways of resistance and for building social and political networks that served their needs in the new country.

Focusing on work of such ignored heroines as Maria Roda, Ernestina Carvallo, Ninfa Baronio, Angela and Maria Bambace, Guglielmo offers compelling counter-stories to previous historical work that has left the contributions of these and many more women in the darkness of American historical registers. With final chapters such as "Anarchist Feminists and the Radical Subculture", "The 1909-1919 Strike Wave and the Birth of Industrial Unionism" and "Red Scare, the Lure of Fascism, and Diasporic Resistance," create a long needed corrective to previous histories of the Italian presence in U.S. labor and politics.

While she doesn't quite get to World War II, which saw greater movement of the Italian American woman into mainstream and formerly male-only positions of public life, Guglielmo exemplary study provides a great foundation for more focused future studies.

Lee Gutkind and Joanna Clapps Herman
Our Roots are Deep with Passion (New York: Other Press)
ISBN:10:1-59051-242-1
June 2007

While you may not be sure just what creative nonfiction is, there is no doubt that the greatest champion of the genre is Professor Lee Gutkind. His pioneering efforts through the journal "Creative Nonfiction" has given new life to the art of writing personal essays. Together with Joanna Clapps Herman, who teaches writing at New York's Center for Worker Education at City College and creative writing in the Graduate Writing Program at Manhattanville College, Gutkind has produced *Our Roots Are Deep with Passion*, which serves as a special issue of Gutkind's journal.

Taking its title from a line in actor Joe Mantegna's sweet and sincere opening essay, *Our Roots* opens with an essay by veteran Louise DeSalvo, whose 'Mbriago," won the $1,000 best essay-award offered by an anonymous donor. While this is certainly not her best work; the stale research on water history and the overused touchstones of Carlo Levi and Pasolini are saved by DeSalvo's defiant sensuality, a trademark of her best storytelling.

Herman's "Words and Rags" is a light and lively rant surveying the landscape of Italian American language centered on the mantra of the "mappin," "the flag of our everyday life," you remember, the kitchen table rag that served as a communal napkin in so many of our families. One of the best essays of the bunch is Edvige Giunta's "The Walls of Gela," a powerful meditation on the lost and found of family through immigration. Giunta's poetic phrasings string together images that sit on a tight line of narrative making this piecework on the levels of art, history, and personal story.

The academic voices of Sandra Gilbert and Marianna DeMarco Torgovnic turn their critical eye inside childhood and adult homes to sift the personal from the political. The seasoned voice of essayist Maria Laurino rings true in "Sacrifice" which riffs on the role personal sacrifice plays in being Italian American. Thanks to Rita Ciresi's "I Heard You the First Time Daddy," and Regina Barecca's "Jealousy, or the Autobiography of an Italian American Woman," Italian Americana won't be seen as taking its pain and suffering too seriously. These essays serve as entertaining antidotes to the irony deficiency so prevalent in much of our public cultural displays.

The collection is composed of mostly new voices, and while the dead grandparents' body count is pretty high, most of the writing stays away from the mawkishly nostalgic to present some fresh insights into Italian American being. This is true of the four men included; Ned Balbo's "My Father's Music," Peter Selgin's "Dagos in Mayberry," James Vescovi's "Mama, Che Cosa Vuoi Faccio?", and Randy-Michael Testa's St. Sebastian in Boston," who all bring interesting insights that are differ from m the usual rough and tumble media portrayals of Italian American men. They all do a good job of going after the father figures and finding new ways of seeing the same old problems between sons and parents. Other honorable mentions include Annie Rachele Lanzillotto's "The Names of Horses," a bitter performance monologue that will keep your ears perked, and Mary Beth Cascetta's "Italian Bridge, a unique take on the Italian wedding.

Our Roots is a worthy purchase, if only to get a better sense of how wide the world of Italian American culture really is, and how so much of it has been lost in the shadows of those sensational stereotypes about which we sometimes complain a bit too much.

Joanna Clapps Herman

The Anarchist Bastard (Albany, NY: State University of New York Press)
ISBN: 978-1-4384-3631-9
October 2011

Joanna Clapps Herman is a veteran storyteller, primarily through non-fiction, who has been teaching her trade for long enough to know that good writing comes to those who work hard. *The Anarchist Bastard* is collection of personal essays, oral history snippets and family snapshots that recount the coming to America of her southern Italian ancestors and their transformation from Italian to 'Merican to Italian American.

The bastard in the stories is her grandfather, an anarchist who takes advantage of his brothers, his wife, and the rest of his family as he finds a way to forget about the poverty of his past. He's a tough guy, unlike the fare we usually get in U.S. media representations, and he is the catalyst for many of the problems his kids and grandkids deny or deal with as they live through wars in their country and sometimes at home.

Herman, a master storyteller, knows well the power of myth and finds ways of attaching her own origin stories to those of writers the likes of Homer. The opening essay "My Homer" sets the tune and pace of these lively accounts of her family's foibles and fun. The opening section is filled with history, humor and analysis that transforms her book education into street wisdom that she passes on to new generations.

Part II, "The Unsayable: The Clapps Family," is filled with all the wonders and warts of her father's side of the family. Telling secrets might not get her warmly welcomed at the next family gathering, but it certainly goes far in showing what can happen if you have the guts to tell the truth according to your point-of-view. She captures childhood confusion and renders it real enough to make adults cringe and wonder just where were the boundaries between youth and adults in this family. Quite effectively the author often steps aside and gives the floor to those who experienced the tales first-hand.

In Part III, "Before and After Tinfoil: The Becce Family," Herman recounts her mother's family's stories and begins with the anarchist bastard himself. Using the same shifts from first person narrator to the voices of those whose stories she is telling, she paints an equally powerful portrait of the other side of the family. Three of the essays that stand out are "Stitching our Voices Together," "Coffee And," and my favorite, "Words and Rags" which deals with her family's dialect, something that she believes keeps her Italian and slows down her from becoming Italian American—something anyone who has used a "mappin" knows all too well.

Part IV, "E' Poi And Then," follows Joanna as she makes her way out of the Connecticut Little Italy and into America where she connects to the intellectual world dominated by the Jewish American world of her husband, something that she does with some hesitation and without losing touch with that ancient world of her tribal upbringing.

The Anarchist Bastard is a virtual workshop in family writing. Family stories can be like family movies—great for those who are in them and boring for those who are not; but that's not the case here. Whether it's a sin, tragedy, party, or accounts of the work they must do to survive in difficult times and places, Herman recreates family events that remind us of our own.

Vincent L. Inserra
C-1 and the Chicago Mob (Bloomington, IN: Xlibris LLC)
ISBN: 978-1-4931-8279-4
June 2015

Chicago's organized crime scene has been played out for years, not so much in films as the famous five families of New York, but certainly in the news; and since the 2007 "Family Secrets" trial, "le cose nostre" of Chicago's Outfit, have headed their inevitable way into the myth that all history, sooner or later becomes. So what do we need with yet another book on the subject?

If you want, like *Dragnet's* Sergeant Joe Friday, just the facts, then you need look no further than Vincent L. Inserra's *C-1 and the Chicago Mob*. Inserra was an eyewitness to the "glory days" of the Outfit. From 1957 until his retirement, Inserra worked in the Chicago Office of the FBI. For thirteen of those years he led the C-1 Organized Crime Squad, and that's where the bulk of his book is centered.

Inserra, a Boston-born son of Italian immigrants served as a fighter pilot in the U.S. Navy during World War Two. He went on to study business at Boston College, and in 1951 he joined the FBI as a Special Agent. His early work in New York involved Soviet Satellite matters. Soon he was reassigned to Chicago to boost their fledgling criminal investigation operations, because, as he writes, "I was of Italian descent" and "I would be able to pronounce the Italian names." After the infamous Appalachian, New York meeting of U.S. gangsters in 1957, the government created the Top Hoodlum Program and the Chicago Office of the FBI became its headquarters, and Inserra became one of its top agents.

The book opens with a short biography of the author's early life growing up in the Roxbury neighborhood of Boston. The Inserras, the father from Sicily and the mother from Naples, had five children, and provided what you might call a normal life for Vincent and his siblings. Like so many young men of his days, Vincent wanted to help out in the war effort; he served as a carrier-based fighter pilot. After the war he continued to fly in the Naval Reserve. From there it was college, then FBI training, and assignments in Chicago where he met the woman he would marry. Then came reassignments to Savannah, Georgia and New York, before he returned to Chicago in 1957.

After this short jaunt through his personal life, the book shifts to his professional activities. The accounts here read more like official reports slightly framed by the contexts in which they were created. Inserra tells, "just the facts." And while all this serves up an incredibly detailed account of the squad's activities, it swerves away from pure storytelling and into more matter-of-fact presentation of reports.

There are details involving investigations from Accardo to Zizzo. A lot of time is spent on the more notorious of Chicago's mobster who's who, like Sam Giancana and the FBI's investigation into the Kennedy assassinations, which Inserra believe had absolutely no connection to the Outfit. In the end, *C-1* becomes a one-sided, though interesting, look behind the scenes of just how the Outfit was stalked and sedated by the federal government.

C-1 is a tribute to all those agents who served in Criminal Squad Number One in Chicago. Back when surveillance depended on shadowing known criminals and setting up eavesdropping equipment in their hangouts, Inserra and his fellow Feds, behind the leadership of J. Edgar Hoover and

Robert Kennedy, wreaked havoc on the lives of those who believed they could get away with murder. If you're an Outfit buff or an amateur sleuth, you'll get what you're looking for in this book.

This is Vincent L. Inserra's first book.

Marisa Labozzetta
Thieves Never Steal in the Rain (Toronto: Guernica Editions)
ISBN: 978-1771830508
August 2012

Thieves Never Steal in the Rain is Marisa Labozzetta's third book of fiction, her second of short stories. These stories differ from her first collection, *At the Copa*, in that they are linked, meaning there are familiar characters and settings throughout the ten stories; this makes the fiction ring like a novel by the time you finish reading them all.

Labozzetta's previous work has garnered critical attention and awards such as a Pushcart Prize for *At the Copa* — also a finalist for the prestigious John Gardner Fiction Award in 2009. One of the stories in this new collection, "Forecast for a Sunny day," won the Watchung Arts Center Award for Short Fiction in 2010. The author carries her award-winning skills to new levels in this work.

Thieves Never Steal in the Rain is available only in electronic format; you need to download it onto your computer (you can get a free Kindle application from Amazon.com) or to your Kindle or I-Pad. This is the first electronic book that I have reviewed, and while you can't beat the cost, there's something about not having the book in hand that is a bit unsettling for an old paper snob like me. For me, this is the downside of "e" books is not being able to talk back through notes; the upside is that you don't have to worry about where you're going to put the book once you're done reading.

In "Villa Foresta," the opening story, Joanna and Elliot, a middle-aged couple who have lost a young daughter to an early death by accident, travel to Italy to get away from it all only to find themselves closer to their daughter than ever before, realizing that grief can't always overcome the loss that caused it. Rosemary and Nate, another middle-aged couple are introduced in "Deluxe Meatloaf," where they meet for a dinner that signals the end of their marriage, something that takes Rosemary, a successful advice columnist, by surprise. Rosemary's answers to her readers often contains a recipe for some food that will aid in dealing with the problem she addresses; without a clue, or a recipe for her own problems, Rosemary deals with this loss by emptying her sorrows in the street outside the restaurant.

Labozzetta is a master at capturing the internal and external forces that bring change into the lives of her characters, and expressing them through a variety of voices. Whether it's self perceived (and obsessed) obesity, as in "Pretty Face" or a mistaken reading of how good others have it, as in "A Perfect Father," the author explores the strengths of her characters so thoroughly that their weaknesses seem natural partners. You can't have the good in life without the bad, and somehow you have to learn how to live a life balancing the two. Some succeed, some fail, but all of her characters teach us much about our own lives.

The female cousins who are the protagonists in each story come together in "Comfort Me, Stranger," to save Rosemary when the depression from her divorce makes it impossible for her to continue her advice column. Joanna, Nancy, Barbara and Angie, all take turns responding to Rosemary's readers, each failing to meet the reader's needs, yet together they succeed in saving their wounded cousin, though everyone is worried about the roommate she takes in to help ease her loneliness.

The final two stories bring us into the world of dealing with aging and dying parents, and in these stories the characters come together to help and sometimes hinder each other as they face new challenges. In this, as in the other stories, Labozzetta reminds us that supernatural and the common provide ways of dealing with the ups and downs of the loves and losses of family life.

Salvatore LaGumina
The Humble and the Heroic: Wartime Italian Americans
    (Amherst, NY: Cambria Press)
ISBN: 0-977-3567-7-9.
May 2007

As we celebrate Memorial Day this year, it might be a good time to take a look around and see how much memory of World War II remains alive and available for transmission into the future.

So much of what we know about World War II has come to us in history books and in the great documentaries that appear regularly on television's History and Biography channels. The problem with most of that knowledge is that it comes to us through or simply about the major figures who seem to have earned all the credit for winning battles and negotiating treaties. If you're lucky you have heard more personalized stories from relatives, neighbors, and perhaps friends who went through it, but the chances are you have never had as thorough a telling of what happened during the war as you will find in Salvatore LaGumina's latest book, *The Humble and the Heroic: Wartime Italian Americans*.

LaGumina, Professor Emeritus and Director of the Center for Italian American Studies at Nassau Community College, is one of the leading historians of the Italian American, experience, especially in New York. His previous works included *Wop: A Documentary History of Anti-Italian Discrimination*, *From Steerage to Suburb: Long Island Italians*, and the encyclopedia project *The Italian American Experience*. In his latest work he takes a position quite different from his usual distanced and objective position as scholar to include his own point-of-view as a participant-observer of the Italian American experience in World War II.

The result is a unique pastiche of scholarship and memoir in this reminiscence of the lives of those Tom Brokaw called "The Greatest Generation".

Story and history from Italian America's elder statesman combine to show how New York's Italians go to war on the battlefronts and at home, and in the process become Americans with a loyalty that will no longer be questioned. While focusing on the larger Italian American effort throughout the country, including the discussion of the unprecedented percentage of Italian American women and men in the armed forces, the "enemy alien status" of many immigrants, and the internment camp experience similar to the Japanese and some German Americans, LaGumina, a 13 year old boy when Pearl Harbor was bombed, tells stories of the effect the war had on the neighborhood and on families. This is the perspective that most histories miss and something LaGumina captures so well.

There is always a risk when an historian begins talking about himself, but in this case, it was a risk well taken. LaGumina pops into this history with an anecdote that helps give a personal perspective to concepts such as poverty, resource rationing, loyalty suspicion, social hostility and war bonds, that are no doubt strange to subsequent generations of Americans.

His section on the heroes is little more than a retelling of what has already been known about the likes of Sergeant John Basilone, the man General MacArthur called the "one man army" and fighter ace Don Gentile, but it is necessary material considering the ambitious scope of LaGumina's project.

LaGumina's contribution is unique in that it covers the socio-political and cultural elements equally without depending too much on the military basis of most World War II histories. These reminiscences form a personalized history full of information accessible to a wide range of readers. So whether you're a veteran of the battlefront or home front, or you know someone who was, this book has something for you and will no doubt, reward students, scholars, and casual readers alike.

Annie Rachele Lanzillotto
L is for Lion: An Italian Bronx Butch Freedom Memoir (Albany, NY: SUNY Press)
ISBN: 978-1438-445250
September 2013

You can take a kid out of the neighborhood, but you can't take the neighborhood out of the kid. Ever hear that saying? I'm asking because it's getting to be used less and less as the old idea of neighborhood, in which people actually cared and took care of each other in small geographically defined urban spaces, disappears; you need to know it to understand this memoir by Bronx native performance artist Annie Rachele Lanzillotto.

Annie, for those who don't know her, is first-of-all, a powerful person who is not confined by most definitions people learn to apply to women who love all people, but prefer their sexual encounters to be with other women. This might turn off those who don't want to be exposed to such lifestyles, but they will be missing out on a truly inspirational story that takes us beyond gender, beyond sexual persuasion, and into the humanity that defines us all. More than a woman, Annie is a human, and her style of humanity is welcomingly infectious. Being around her might make you feel uncomfortable, especially if you've never been pushed beyond the limits of an institutionally refined and educated sense of humanity. But her presence will challenge you to think and act in ways that ring true to what's deep inside us all, those forces that culture sometimes helps us repress.

Annie's formal education is something that worried her grandmother, the Italian immigrant who taught Annie so much about life that challenged her private school education shaped sensibilities. Granma Rose, who hailed from Bari, is one tough woman, who calls her granddaughter "Educationa girl," partly to mock and challenge her to think beyond her formal schooling, and partly to honor Annie for achieving something she herself could never have.

The key to this memoir is not what Annie experiences, but how she processes it, Bronx accent and all. Hers is a story about healing, first herself through a few bouts with cancer, and then others, her mother's heart surgery, and the illnesses of so many others. Her most challenging encounter is her father's post-traumatic stress from his World War II combat experiences. That stress, and her father's inability to deal with it, forces her mother to leave the man she loved simply to survive. Yet, Annie never abandons the man who terrorized her life and the lives of those she loved. Instead, she confronts it all in a way that teaches us all how not to run from our fears.

Another lesson here is how to live with your parent's fears and keep them from becoming your own. Annie does this so well by first gathering the information she needs to process understanding of what makes people in her life behave the way they do. Her model here is her own teenage battle with Hodgkin's disease, something she learns about just as she starts her own life in college. She defies all odds because she gathers the information she needs to heal herself, then she goes about educating others, even her doctors. When her mother gets hit with open-heart surgery, it is Annie who tackles the healing process. And while she can't save her father, because he refuses to save himself, she never stops loving him and deals with his disease until he dies.

Annie's is a liberating story, not only in what happens to her, but also in the way she tells it. There are no precise and separate chapters; though the book is organized into chronologically based sections: Bronx Tomboy, Educationa Girl, Kimosabe, How to Cook a Heart, and Annie's Parts, each is composed of short pieces that come at us the way our lives our lived, in bits and pieces that only become whole when we reflect back and recount them to others. *L is for Lion* is an extraordinary telling of experiences ordinary in the life of a Bronx Butch.

Garibaldi M. LaPolla
The Grand Gennaro (New Brunswick, NY: Rutgers University Press)
ISBN: 978-0-8135-4569-1.
June 2010

There are not many Italian American works of literature written in the 1930s that remain in print, and this leads to an historical cultural amnesia that keeps the best of our culture from outshining such warts as *Jersey Shore*. Sure, we have Pietro di Donato's *Christ in Concrete* and John Fante's *Wait Until Spring Bandini*, but there are only two of the dozens of works that, if read by all Americans, would go a long way in moving us beyond the usual stereotypes. Thanks to Rutgers Press and its MELA series (Multi-Ethnic Literatures of America) edited by Amritjit Singh, C. Lok Chua, and Carla L. Peterson, another Italian American classic has reappeared.

Garibaldi M. LaPolla's *The Grand Gennaro* is the story of one Gennaro Accuci, an immigrant from Calabria who is determined to "make America" no matter the cost. Gennaro risks everything, including his family's name, in order to change his lot in life from poor immigrant to rich American — everything, that is, except for his gold hoop earrings — pierced by his father in the old country. What happens to those earrings, and to the man who refuses to take them off, makes for one great drama rendered through clear and lively prose.

Set in during the turn of the 19th and early 20th centuries, the novel captures life in the New York Little Italy as none has before or since. LaPolla renders New York skyline scenes as impressionist paintings and neighborhoods as Jacob Riis photos; in this way he sets a mood while advancing the plot.

Gennaro arrives in New York's Italian Harlem and gets a job working with Rocco the junk man. Soon he becomes partners with his boss and in no time (and with no concern for his actions) pushes Rocco out. While he makes America at a relatively early age, it is what he does with it, and what it does to him, that makes the novel a classic.

LaPolla is neither nostalgic nor naïve in the way he approaches his story. Gennaro, as cruel as he can be at times is nearly always aware of what he is doing and acts according to what he believes are old country values. The author devotes a great deal of time to the women who enter Gennaro's life, often using them to soften his crude antics and elevate him beyond his often despicable behavior. There's a sort of Dante/Beatrice aspect to Gennaro's relationship with women; those he doesn't drag down are able to lift him to higher ways of thinking and being.

The novel is a treasure house of the phrases and sounds of the Italian language and life. LaPolla captures immigrant voices in comprehensible ways, enabling us to listen to voices from a past century as though they were downloadable recordings. From daily life in the rag picking business to the local American and Italian feste, Italian Harlem comes alive as we watch Gennaro move from rag picker to business owner to real estate magnate. Things go well for the lucky immigrant until he falls victim to the old saying "what goes around comes around" when he's not paying attention.

The edition was edited with an introduction by Steven J. Belluscio, a professor of English at the Borough of Manhattan Community College. Belluscio clearly annotates the Italian used along with other references that might hamper readers not familiar with the period. The introduction is just what you need to have set up a great context for reading. Belluscio rightly compares it to F. Scott Fitzgerald's *Great Gatsby* and provides us with insight into the formal and stylistic elements that make this novel an American classic. He also gives us, for the first time, some biographical insights into the life of the author. All in all the project represents exactly what needs to be done with many other out-of-print Italian American novels.

Maria Laurino
The Italian Americans (New York: W.W. Norton & Company)
ISBN: 978-0393241297
February 2015

Many books have been produced in both popular and academic formats attempting to synthesize the rich and varied stories that make up what has come to be called Italian American history. For years, the most successful of these has been Jerre Mangione and Ben Morreale's *La Storia: Five Centuries of the Italian American Experience*, published in 1993. While *La Storia* served as a decent starting point for those who wished to study Italian American culture, in time, its many weaknesses betrayed its usefulness. Students and scholars alike have been waiting for something new that would not only update developments in U.S. history, but also fill in the lifestyle, gender and historical gaps created in that first great leap into making what Van Wyck Brooks coined as "a usable past," in his 1915 *America's Coming of Age*.

The Italian Americans, while not a candidate for replacing *La Storia* in history classes, does provide us with a new view of the same materials covered in most earlier histories. The great difference is Laurino's lean, journalistic style and her penchant for covering the darker side of Italian American history that sees print in only a handful of the best of studies of Italian American culture.

Laurino's captivating style renews even the most mundane information while covering the usual topics found in previous histories.

As in any attempt to commodify an entire culture one place in print, there is more left out than included. While not deep in substance, Laurino's broad overviews set up possibilities for future, in-depth discoveries. Those who want more, and everyone should, can consult her adequate bibliography to learn about the vast cultural presence forged by Italian American writers and critics, artists and independent filmmakers where her coverage is especially light.

One of the strengths of this book is the acknowledgment of her inability to get it all done in one shot. Her ability to shed light on some of the more unknown and obscure aspects of Italian American culture should be applauded as she enables readers to move beyond the superficial conclusions that have been drawn from more popular presentations that have distorted the imaginary and limited the ability of most Americans to grasp the larger good done by the common citizen of Italian descent. As she writes: "Myths about Italian-American culture run deep into the fabric of American life, obscuring the complicated, nuanced, centuries-long story of the Italian-American experience that demands to be told. One of the goals of this book—alongside telling this history—is to tease the myth from reality and uncover a more complicated story and deeper truths."

Designed and written to accompany John Maggio's four-part PBS supported documentary film, from which Laurino's book takes its title, this history is a pastiche of Laurino's essays joined to well-printed archival photos and illustrations, original documents including newspaper accounts, letters (including a few written by "Black Hand" extortionists), magazine articles, book excerpts, and brief interviews with the likes of Gay Talese, Dion, David Chase and John Turturro. The result is a beautifully designed document that is not only worthy of coffee table permanence, but one that rewards close reading. There is more to our story than meets these pages, but together with Maggio's video, we have ways of moving beyond the stereotypes and into a greater knowledge of the rich stories that make up the contributions of the Americans of Italian descent. If you have only one book in your home library on Italian American culture, make sure it's Laurino's.

Old World Daughter, New World Mother: An Education in Love and Freedom
   (New York: W.W. Norton)
ISBN: 978-0-393-05728-7
March 2010

You can tell that since her first book, *Were You Always Italian*, journalist Maria Laurino has done a lot of thinking about what it means to be an American of Italian descent. In this new book, there's none of the hesitancy of identifying completely with her Italian background that marked her earlier thinking. And while she hasn't become a complete Born-Again Italian, she has learned enough from her past and her research to put that heritage to good use in *Old World Daughter, New World Mother*.

Divided into two sections, "Daughters" and "Mothers," this book is an extended argument on how we can put Old world thinking to use in changing the way we view American life. Comparing her life to her mother's and her grandparents', Laurino finds that the more she tried to get away from her past when she was young, the more it came back to her when she became a mother.

One of the most illuminating sections comes early as she surveys the way she became a feminist by running away from everything her mother and grandmother had been and done. While earlier Italian American women lived by the ways they sacrificed their own needs and wants to support the men and children in their lives, the new generation of women were able to pursue their own dreams. "For better or worse, Italian Americans think about personal sacrifice differently than many Americans, viewing it as they do through a prism of their particular culture and past. Life and sacrifice were synonymous . . ."

As she moves through her career as a journalist and speechwriter for a New York City mayor, she experiences her own challenges and successfully establishes herself as an independent career woman. However, along the way she starts to wonder whether the price paid for independence—increased stress, less family interaction, and the abandonment of proverbial wisdom—is worth the rewards of professional success. She questions feminist ideas "the original feminist position paradoxically championed the rights of women while failing to satisfy the needs of mothers and children."

By the time she gets married and has a child she realizes that in spite of how far she veered from the paths of previous generations, there was something inside that began to emerge: "I began to feel very Italian, that is, within me a deeply protective mamma was emerging who seemed ready to dictate the course of my new life." From her problematic pregnancy on through the early years of caring for her child, she investigates the medical problems and social situations she encounters. Drawing material from major studies, journal articles and interviews, she creates in interesting investigative report that ultimately argues for a return to some of the cultural ways that she had earlier abandoned.

While most of the writing is comfortably clear, there are a number of weaker moments, when she does not, as Ezra Pound would say "kill the little darlings" of her prose, such as when she echoes Erica Jong with the phrase "fear of frying," or Billy Joel with the lines "you Catholic girls start much too late," and an irritating overworking of the metaphor of *vino veneretto*: "Women need to tap the potential of Old World truths that sit before us corked and untouched, waiting for a new way to pour forth." But these are mere editorial lapses in a work that challenges the ways many of us have become 'mericans.

Laurino suggests that Third-wave feminism can utilize a synthesis of the characteristics found in Mary Tyler Moore and Livia Soprano to regain a sense of what's "missing in contemporary American culture: a deep-rooted ethic of care, a belief in human beings as something other than human capital, and a view of life that's isn't first and foremost shaped by economic transactions."

Her message is timely in these days as a new president tries to change old ways of thinking about how we care about each other. That once great sense of American independence, creating competition that carries forth beyond the economy, could be tempered through a return to more communal ways of thinking so that we find ourselves saying, "Yes, we care!"

Frank Lentricchia

The Morelli Thing (Toronto: Guernica Editions)
ISBN-978-1-77183-029-4
April 2016

The third installment of Frank Lentricchia's Eliot Conte mystery series, following *The Accidental Pallbearer* and *The Dog Killers*, finds the ex-professor turned private eye a stay-at-home father to a newborn daughter. Baby Ann, the result of his cohabitation with Catherine Cruz, is in his care and keeps him at his wit's end. Without much of a track record in the father business, Eliot struggles to keep the kid fed, in clean diapers, and not crying as he muddles around his Utica home, waiting for Catherine to return from a visit to her older daughter. When he gets a call from Caruso's Café telling him the news, he begins to sizzle.

Victor Bocca, a local lout and angry old man smashed the guitar of one Angel Moreno, after the seventeen year old uses this new gift from his adopted father Eliot to amuse Utica's Golden Boys, local retirees, as they debate the most famous unsolved crime in Utica history, the 1947 murder of Fred Morelli. Assumed all along to be a mob hit, Angel ruins the old men's theories as he presents evidence he's managed to get through use of his superhuman skills as a computer hacker that links Morelli to none other than Thomas E. Dewey, the famous New York crime fighter turned politician. Angel, home from college, must have struck a wrong chord for Bocca to have behaved so violently, and leaves the café to sulk in his room. Eliot seeks vengeance for the wrong done to his son, but before he can enact whatever physical response his twisted mind can conceive, he finds Victor's body sprawled over his front stoop; someone more professionally prepared than Eliot, got there first, yet Eliot will be suspect of the crime until he can prove he had nothing to do with it.

With this plot, Lentricchia takes us on another wild ride through the streets of Utica, New York, as wild man Eliot, part Sherlock Holmes, more Dirty Harry, flits about town in an effort to keep his family alive and together. Angel, whose family was murdered in the last novel, now is Eliot's charge. Taking care of a newborn, and this genius computer whiz home from the Ivy league school that awarded him a major in computer science before he even takes a class, is more than Eliot can handle. Under the stress, he drifts toward the old habits that got the best of him in the past, and keeps him from finding normal work.

Lentricchia has centered this novel around an actual unsolved murder of one Fred Morelli, who's immigrant father had his cigar business busted by the state for withholding sales tax, an act that drives Fredo to the dark side of Italian power. With punchy dialogue and fast-paced action, Lentricchia keeps the story moving and the plot from giving itself away. His sleuth is someone you love to hate and are afraid to love, and yet, you can't help but wonder just how will Eliot get out of this one. While the solution is ingenious, the action makes us think, could this be the end of Lentricchia's detective work? What could Eliot Conte possibly do next if he must stay in Utica as he reaches the age when health problems arrive unexpectedly to normal seniors, not to mention those who are trouble magnets? And just how much mystery can even a powerful writer such as Lentricchia draw from one small American city?

The Dog Killer of Utica (Brooklyn, NY: Melville House)
ISBN-978-1-61219-773-3
November 2014

    This second installment in this mystery series doesn't presume that you've read the first, *The Accidental Pallbearer*, but if you have, then you're in for more of the same thrills and chills. *The Dog Killer of Utica* picks up where *Pallbearer* leaves off.

    Conte, now in his late 50s is living with Catherine Cruz, the Utica detective he met on a case, in a bungalow that came from his share of his late father's estate. He's returned to teaching American literature in the local college, focused on working out his body through grueling exercises, and his mind, through an ongoing obsession with Herman Melville. He's still struggling with the demons that drove him to drink and continue to drive him to distraction. And he does pretty well until the radio reports that his best friend lies in a hospital, in grave condition from gunshot wounds.

    Conte thinks he knows who the shooter was, but then, when his liquor storeowner gets it next, and after some of the local dogs, and people close to him are attacked, he is driven to doubt and back into his old profession. That's when the demons reappear. He takes this crime spree personally as the body toll of innocents piles higher than the winter snow and the number of suspects rises.

    Eliot's past is riddled with acts of rage and vengeance that lead to violent often vigilante acts that all become the building blocks of this mystery. With each day, Eliot creeps back to his old, self-destructive ways, driving everyone out of his life except for the Mexican boy next door, who reminds Eliot that he was not a good father and who gives him a chance to redeem himself. But not before he solves the mystery that has taken hold of Utica.

Lentricchia's gutsy and sometimes-gory scenes are brilliantly composed. With suspense tightly balanced on the reality of everyday actions, you never know what's going to happen next, and this keeps the narrative alive. Conte is no mastermind like Sherlock Holmes; he's just your average, everyday lout (edgier than Colombo) whose keen sense of interpretation, honed on literary investigations, enables him to establish motive before all the evidence turns up.

There's more to this novel than solving the mystery of murders. Lentricchia establishes a sense of place in language that makes this a literary mystery, as in this description of a local diner. "What pleases Conte about Toma's is its seamlessly drab appearance. The weak light. The crowded space. A ceiling that would give some but not a great deal of clearance to a professional basketball player. The smell of coffee, too long roasted. Toma's—a token of the East Utica that was, where he discovered two months ago that it was possible, however briefly, to lay by his troubles."

When immigrants move in next door, and teach Eliot how to turn his back yard into a dream garden, a second mystery is built that reaches deep into Conte's past. There are other twists as when one of Eliot's students, a Bosnian Muslim, gets himself in trouble with Homeland Security, and a local radio star reveals a surprising secret. Eliot chases down answers only to find out that he doesn't know everything, and these developments keep "The Dog Killer of Utica" from becoming a run-of-the-mill mystery, turning it into a shocking and simple story of life.

The Accidental Pallbearer (Brooklyn, NY: Melville House)
ISBN: 978-1-61219-171-3
May 2013

Move over Lisa Scottoline, David Baldacci and Robert Ferrigno, there's a new Italian American mystery writer on the scene. Frank Lentricchia, who by now has produced more pages of fine writing in fiction than he had during his stellar career as a literary critic, has moved into the detective/thriller genre with *The Accidental Pallbearer*.

A far cry from his earlier more literary fiction, but not too far from his more recent works like *The Italian Actress* and *The Sadness of Antonioni*, this new novel is a tight, twisted and totally engaging read that follows the life of private detective Eliot Conte.

Conte is a middle-aged former professor who once dangled a university provost out of his office window in a fit of rage. When he returns home to Utica, New York after his expulsion from UCLA, his political kingpin father Silvio, who prefers to be called "Big Daddy" by those he controls, sets him up in a comfortable home only to earn his son's disdain. The father/son tension keeps the plot on a tightrope that takes readers over the working class terrain of upstate New York and keeps Lentricchia's take on the genre grounded in a gritty reality making Conte's strange work habits seem not only normal but necessary.

Conte is friends with all the right, and often, all the wrong people, and he has a hard time telling the difference between the two. In very unconventional ways, he gets the job done when he stumbles into a web of crime that could very well have his own father at its center. Silvio, the man who made most of the local and even some national politicos bend to his will, cannot have his way with his son, something he regrets more and more as he nears his own grave. When father and son come together in the old man's hospital room, Eliot learns more than he bargained for and begins to understand that his old man might not be so bad for a gangster. The soul searching that accompanies his clue searching is key to the big difference this mystery has from most others.

But Eliot isn't so concerned about his father as he is about the rising death rate in the Utica neighborhood. Seems each stone he turns in search of an alleged serial rapist gets used against those he interrogates. It gets to the point where he could easily, because of the way he works, become victim and suspect. Conte is as cool and as crude as detectives come — two qualities he uses to his advantage as he solves crimes that come his way as he attempts to do a favor for his brother-like friend Antonio Robison, the city's first black police chief. The life he lives is not one to envy, but certainly one to watch, especially as he makes his way toward a new love while investigating one of the area's oldest unsolved crimes, one that just might involve the very people he knows and loves.

Lentricchia's invention is certainly original and harbors a plot that's worthy of the best detective minds. Sure, there's the usual Italian organized crime element at work in these pages, but not in the old hackneyed ways. Sure there's a major mob hit that wipes out the area's dons in one fell swoop at an old lady's funeral, but Conte's investigation into history uncovers more than what you expect. Once again, Lentricchia has forged a fiction that has guts. There's a depth in this novel that will satisfy even the more reluctant mystery readers, but it's not for feint-hearted mystery readers who love red herrings. With nary a bump in the prose, Lentricchia keeps it real while building enough suspense to keep the brain clicking and the pages turning.

The Sadness of Antonioni (Albany, NY: State University of New York Press)
ISBN: 978-1-4383-3912-9
January 2012

Is it just me, or is Frank Lentricchia's writing getting better with every book? His latest novel, *The Sadness of Antonioni*, is filled with all the things that make for a good read while maintaining the high quality that makes for Literature with a capital "L"; this is a book that pleases readers, students, and scholars alike.

First of all, there are characters we can care about; then there's a plot that is steady without being obese or intrusive; and finally all this is served in a style of writing that takes what Antonioni did with time and space in film and applies it to the two dimensions of the page. You don't need to have seen Antonioni's films to like this book, but if you have, you do to get into the depths of art that Lentricchia reaches with words. You also don't need to have read any of Lentricchia's earlier novels to enjoy *The Sadness*, but if you have read the *Italian Actress*, the curiosity raised about the strange career of the over-the-hill, avant-garde filmmaker and pitiful professor, Jack Del Piero, will be satisfied, as will your moral sense of fictional justice.

In this new novel, Lentricchia gives us Hank Morelli, one of those whiz-kid graduate students who created a genius thesis and then tries to build a career upon and around it. While this rookie professor's study of Antonioni's films creates new ways of seeing the artist, Morelli can't avoid a life that could easily have been an Antonioni film. This is the result of Lentricchia's literary mastery at work. He takes a character's strength, reveals all the weaknesses about it, and then sits back as they both fight over control of the person they inhabit.

When Hank falls in love with a thirty-year old Wendy's server, we can't help but wonder just what this writer is up to. Turns out Hank and Jenny have connections between them that go deep into their past and right through Ritrona's Bakery and Café in Stormbridge, a local New England college town where Hank lives and teaches. Cliff Ritrona, the bakery's owner, has an interesting past that includes knowledge of how Hank's grandfather was murdered and how Jenny became an orphan. This all comes together in mysterious ways that keep the pages turning, and the reader yearning for an answer to it all.

But Hank is not the only one with darkness in his past. His girlfriend, and later his wife, has had her own run-ins with the underworld that jeopardize her safety in ways that make Hank helpless and Cliff, with his big heart and street smarts, necessary.

Told in both first and third person, from various character's points of view, *The Sadness of Antonioni*, takes risks that include heavy close reading of Antonioni's films, intrusions of organized crime, and the strangest of allusions to films like Hitchcock's *Psycho*. The risks pay off in a big way when we get to the end of Morelli's career and learn from the very last lecture he gives, that actions speak louder than words, something Antonioni showed us throughout his films.

Lentricchia is not afraid of death violent, peaceful or perverted, and uses it in his art as a relief against which mundane life acts and fantastic dreams struggle to make life matter. All in all, *The Sadness* is a challenging work that will make you think more than most of what you've read lately, and deeper than most other writers trying to make literature matter in today's image-bloated world.

The Book of Ruth (Edmonds, WA: Ravenna Press)
ISBN: 0-9766593-5-2
March 2006

In his latest fiction Frank Lentricchia creates a story more traditional than any he's written yet. *The Book of Ruth* is a timely tale of nervous love, the artist's life, and what happens when the inner world of intuition and inspiration gives in to the outer world of reputations and relationships. While not an historical novel in itself, *The Book of Ruth* does deal with some key figures of U.S. history since 1950. Taking a page out of a few DeLillo novels such as *Libra* and *Mao II*, Lentricchia fashions a plot involving Fidel Castro, the Kennedy brothers, and Saddam Hussein with one Ruth Cohen, an amateur photographer and one-book wonder. *Cuban Stories*, her photographic portrait of the 1950s' newly Communist Cuba, made her famous enough so she has never had to do another book for the rest of her life.

One day, nearly 30 years after that publication, a magazine editor gets the bright idea to track her down and make her an offer she won't refuse. It seems the "New Yorker" wants to get an exclusive photo spread of Iraq and Saddam Hussein, and have Ruth do what she did to Castro's Cuba. In order to get her out of retirement and into Iraq prior to the Gulf War to work her visual magic on Saddam, they need to up the ante by including a promise of fame to her experimental novelist husband Thomas Lucchesi, Jr.

The couple lives reclusively on an unmapped lake in upstate New York, land willed to her by one John D. Rockefeller. It seems that Cohen has been the darling of many powerful men, mistress to a few, and now faithful wife to Lucchesi who writes edgy novels that few people read and even fewer understand, yet Lucchesi is admired by the likes of French philosopher

Michel Foucault. The academic/novelist is obsessed with trying to stay alive and well and so is a worrywart who living light in his fiction and quite heavy outside of it. The "New Yorker" editor knows that in order to get Ruth to take the job Lucchesi will have to be a part of it, so along with a lucrative offer to the photographer, she offers to republish all of Lucchesi's previous books supported by substantial publicity. Ruth knows that Thomas really wants this, but he's too proud to let her know it; she gives in and the two head off for Iraq.

This work reveals a more refined style than we've seen in Lentricchia's two previous novels. The plot is more traditional and the action more evenly paced. We also see a bit more insight into the role being Italian American plays helping a writer delve into the more edgy and experimental aspects of art. When Lucchesi takes Ruth back to his old Utica neighborhood, she understands her husband's statement that "a male novelist is driven by nostalgia to return in his imagination to the place of his childhood". But the most interesting action takes place in Iraq, a place Lentricchia's never been, yet draws in brilliant detail and in such a way as to make us realize that reality recreated is nothing without a strong imagination.

Lentricchia has perhaps written his most poignant prose to create a fiction that comments well on contemporary U.S. culture. It many ways this is a mainstream novel and yet it is published by the smallest press to ever produce a Lentricchia book. As poet Jay Parini says on the back cover blurb, *The Book of Ruth* "deserves a wide audience".

Les Leopold
The Man Who Hated Work and Loved Labor: The Life and Times of Tony Mazzocchi
    (White River Junction, VT: Chelsea Green Press)
ISBN: 978-1-933392-64-6
September 2008

One of the keys to *The Man Who Hated Work and Loved Labor: The Life and Times of Tony Mazzocchi* is the way biographer Les Leopold brings in the history and politics that made and were made by this leading figure in the American labor movement. Leopold is thorough, if at times relentless, in bringing us the incredible intricacies of the life of one man who had touched so many and the connections to the larger social-history in which Mazzocchi operated.

If you don't know Tony Mazzocchi, then you're probably in the majority. Historian Howard Zinn called him "one of the unsung, unnoticed heroes of the American working class." The grandson of Italian immigrants, Mazzochi was born in 1926 and grew up in New York City's Bensonhurst Little Italy. His training as a leader began early when "he headed up a pack of tough kids" in his neighborhood. Traditional academics didn't do much for him and he ended up in a maritime vocational school. He left school as soon as he was legally able and started to work.

When World War II broke he lied about his age and enlisted. A veteran of the Battle of the Bulge, Tony saw intense combat, participated in the occupation of Germany, and was one of the earliest to view the effects of the infamous Buchenwald concentration camp. Here he connected his family's concern with racism to the larger world and returned solid in his conviction that things had to change.

A number of historical themes run throughout Mazzocchi's life. One of the most prevalent is civil rights. His progressive thinking and acting parents shaped his moral sense of the world to move beyond institutional foundations to champion the humanitarian needs of all people; he took this strong family sense of justice-for-all into the world of organized labor.

True equality and justice, Mazzocchi believed, would only come if men could find ways of doing as little work as possible. "He drew a strong distinction between corporate work and what he called, 'redefined work.' Corporate work included traditional factory jobs and menial service jobs. 'Redefined' work was getting paid to do creative things, to promote social change, to think and to grow."

From the moment he started his first job, until his dying day, Tony fought to make the worker matter, the workplace safer, and to offer every worker one a chance to be educated and heard. His life work was a part of such national political activity as the American Communist Party, presidential campaigns for the likes of Henry Wallace and Robert Kennedy, and attempts to form third party alternatives such as the Labor Party.

Never a card carrying Commie, Mazzocchi sympathized with their efforts to change American labor, but was turned off by the way doctrine would cloud social vision and stymie direct action that mattered to the worker. He preferred to get his information directly from the worker and act from there.

Mazzocchi's union activity spanned his entire life. President of Local 8-149, he spent most of his life in the Oil Chemical, and Atomic Workers International Union (OCAW) — then the Paper, Allied-Industrial, Chemical and Energy Workers (PACE) — where he served as Executive Board member, Legislative Director, Health and Safety Director, Vice-President and Secretary-Treasurer. He worked with Ralph Nader, championed work safety through the Karen Silkwood murder, and pioneered countless changes in workers' health and safety.

Leopold has produced a fitting record of and tribute to the man who gave his life to the American worker, and left a legacy that affected us all.

Maria Lisella
Amore on Hope Street (www.finishinglinepress.com)
ISBN: 978-1-59924-533-1
December 2010

Amore on Hope Street is Maria Lisella's second poetry chapbook to appear in 2009; over two dozen gems come in sections on immigrant similarities and clashes, the family here and gone, and travels abroad and inside relationships. Lisella excels in both lyric and narrative forms, bringing the real to surface though things like a young girl's pierced ears, and sometimes through the sur-reality of a Venetian fog. Through skills of framing her subjects she makes the past seem present and the present seem past, creating poetry you want to read and reread.

Billy Lombardo
The Logic of a Rose: Chicago Stories (Kansas City, MO: BkMk Press)
ISBN: 1886157502.
November 2005

Winner of the G.S. Sharat Chandra Prize for Short Fiction, *The Logic of a Rose* brings together eight Chicago stories by Billy Lombardo, and all but the title story have appeared in such publications as *Story Quarterly, Other Voices* and *River Oak Review*.

Lombardo tells new stories about the old Chicago Bridgeport neighborhood of the 1970s, home of the mayor, Chicago White Sox, Dressel's bakery and the Bellapani family. Petey, along with his mother and father, who delivers for Dressel's on the weekends, is the focus of most of the stories, and his coming of age in the city is as good as any you've read before. At his best, Lombardo reads like a nice Nelson Alrgen; he creates a character whose wisdom comes not from the tough breaks in life, but from breaking through the tough things life throws his way. Everyone, whether suburban or city bred can relate to these meditations on ordinary occurrences.

When you belong to the working class, your job is you and mostly what you have to talk about. But Lombardo's characters are always more than their jobs. Learning how to work, how to do things the right way, whether it's mopping a floor or delivering papers is a training ground for learning to live right.

A first-sucker punch in the stomach, the accidentally hurting of a playmate, the reactive violence, the terror of a fire out of control and the peace of a neighbor's welcome, are all portrayed by Lombardo with the patience of a painter of miniatures. "Nickels" will take you back to the times when kids and adults pitched pennies and everyone kept an eye out for neighbors' kids. "Blessed is the Fruit" uses the life and death of a cherry tree planted by the neighbors, the Romanos, to explain how old cultures can renew and old neighborhood. When "The Wallace Playlot", where boys can be boys without parents around, disappears one summer, no one is there to save the neighborhood from the new housing that will change it forever.

In "The Hills of Laura" we learn that there are things in life that one must experience even if it's only through others. With "Mrs. Higgins's Heart and the Smell of Fire," Lombardo masters the way sensory perception gives birth to language; smells are stories and the fire of Dressel's bakery, which destroys Petey's family apartment and nearly takes them with it, leaves them with a story to tell and a smell that won't let them forget it

The title story, "The Logic of a Rose," a beautiful account of first love and how a strange birthmark can turn in to a treasure.

In "The Thing about Swing" we move away from Petey, though we might see the protagonist of this story as Petey later in life. College boy Danny has a system for washing his clothes in the local laundromat that works well until a co-ed interferes. Danny and the girl check each other out only to realize that this is not the first time they have met.

The Logic of a Rose: Chicago Stories is a refreshingly new look at a way of living that has shaped a whole generation. Lombardo's prose is flawlessly disciplined so that what it doesn't give you, you learn to take from it. Endings, for example, are frayed, the way life really is. There are no neatly knotted bows atop these stories. And while you may have lived all this before, you haven't read it the way Lombardo tells it.

Robert Lombardo
The Black Hand: Terror by Letter in Chicago (Urbana-Champaign, IL: University of Illinois Press)
ISBN: 978-0-252-03488-6
November 2010

Besides being excellent history, Robert Lombardo's *The Black Hand: Terror by Letter in Chicago* provides the definitive argument that this form of crime was not imported from Italy. In fact, he sees it as a natural outgrowth of experiences and events rooted in American society. Lombardo has diligently sifted through newspaper accounts, police reports, trial transcripts to separate myth from mystery, fact from fiction producing a viable account of why Italian Americans have been burdened with the Mafia stereotype for so long.

If the truth is that Italians have always been underrepresented in crime statistics, then how does it happen that the mere mention of organized crime will bring to mind slick Italians slicing throats as though they were sticks of pepperoni? Lombardo blames it on the alien conspiracy theory perpetrated mostly powerfully by the Kefauver Commission in the 1950s (our earliest reality television) resulting in "forever tying Italian Americans to organized crime. Lombardo favors the ethnic-succession theory that explains Italian presence in organized crime as a means of social advancement, and spends the better part of the book making a strong case for his thesis.

Lombardo, a professor of sociology and criminal Justice at Loyola University, comes to academia after a 35 year career in city and county police work, and that experience has served him well both in researching and communicating the results of his work. It is clear that beyond history and sociology Lombardo employs a great understanding of legal procedures and their jargon, enhancing this history beyond the usual replication of what is found in written accounts. His interpretations are keen and original.

He opens with a general overview of the history of Italian immigration to Chicago, setting up the context for his study of Black Hand crimes. Subsequent chapters cover the crimes and various attempts to deal with them, first by the Italian American community through something called the White Hand Society, and then by the Chicago Police through the Black Hand Squad. The last three chapters deal with crimes attributed to Black Hand activities during the Prohibition era—a time during which Chicago organized crime flourished, examinations of the causes of Black Hand crime, and the role that the American mass media played in creating the connection between Italian Americans and Mafia.

His well-written and documented accounts of Black Hand crimes all build toward his claim that the mass media of the time did nothing but perpetrate and perpetuate crime myths "that typify reality to make comprehensible what is inherently complicated and obscure". In other words, in a rush to grab attention and sell products, the media never did the rigorous investigation and interpretation of crimes that occurred in Italian neighborhoods, instead, lumping them all into the real of a Black Hand that never existed as organized crime. In "The Social Construction of Deviance," his final and I think best chapter, Lombardo attributes the connection between Black Hand crimes and Italian Americans to a series of U.S. newspaper articles that appeared as early as 1890.

This is a book that needed to be written two generations ago, one that everyone needs to read today to make up for lost time. Lombardo has done a great service not only to Chicago history, but also to Italian Americans throughout the United States.

Lorraine Paolucci Macchello

The Dowry: Legacies to an Italian American Daughter (San Francisco: Tramondi Publishing)
ISBN: 0-615-12511-5
January 2006

It used to be that when a woman got married her family would present the husband's family with gifts, and that often the family that could provide the dowry were not able to marry off their daughters. While times have certainly changed, the gifts that one family gives another continue on in the way they shape the two who are getting married. This is the idea behind Lorraine Paolucci Macchello's first book, *The Dowry: Legacies to an Italian American Daughter*. Through a compilation of 27 sketches, an epilogue, and a final note, we come to learn the story of Carlo and Maria Paolucci as they emigrate from Pesaro, Italy in the early 1920s to the United States, and proceed to raise a daughter in the San Francisco area of California.

In the old days, the family's stories would live on through the storytellers, and when that oral tradition worked well, we didn't need to have the written word to remember how people moved from one place to another, from one job to another, from one demeanor to another. But as old neighborhoods gave way to new inhabitants, and families started to depend on holidays or yearly reunions to recall the past and catch up on changes, the methods of passing on stories needed to change as well. In many ways, *Dowry* is a good model for how each of us might compile the stories that make up the histories of our families.

As a testament to that oral tradition, Macchello begins many of her chapters with a proverb that in some way relates to the theme of the story she is telling. The opening story, appropriately entitled *Dowry* tells of the *biancheria* that has survived from her mother's trousseau. Through the "everyday things one needed to run a household and the personal items of clothing" that are passed on through the family, such as handmade blankets "spun from the yarn" of the family's own sheep, hand embroidered tablecloths and napkins, Macchello comes to know the grandmother she never met. From these objects and the stories she's told when she's young, she recreates a rich family history.

From Pesaro, Italy to North Beach San Francisco and back to Italy in later years, the stories cover geographical spaces traversed and inhabited by the Paolucci family through three generations. Macchello fondly recalls the efficient system women used to hang their laundry out to dry on "Backyard Clotheslines." "Sunday Picnics" and "The Ranch" recall times when the family would get away from city life to breathe fresh air and harvest natural foods.

While the greatest value of these recollections will serve the author's family now and in years to come the better essays here spark the reader's own memory every now and then. The weaker ones tend to be little more than home movies that seem to repeat information we already learned in earlier sections. Fortunately these are few, and a good editing would have eliminated them. For the most part though, *Dowry* is made up of good, clean writing, that, while falling short of achieving literary status, never drag us into the personal pomposity that plague many family histories.

A large section of the book follows Macchello's mother from widowhood to the nursing home. During this time we watch as the daughter becomes the mother to the woman who once mothered her. Fortunately the two of them get to travel back to the family's ancestral home in Italy and in the process learn to appreciate each other in new ways. *Dowry* ends on a nice note as the author tells how her grandchildren now have come to make use of what she's been able to pass on to them, and the author, once known as the daughter of Carlo Paolucci, the wife of Mac, is now hailed as the Grandmother of Nicholas. This makes us wonder just when a woman gets to be known as her self in this family, but Macchello is happy to have been the one to have captured all this rich life in words.

Elise Magistro
Behind Closed Doors (New York: The Feminist Press)
ISBN: 978-1-55861-553-6
December 2007

Maria Messina's stories are among the jewels of early 20th century Italian literature and come to us in a beautiful English translation by Elise Magistro. *Behind Closed Doors: 'Her Father's House' and other Stories of Sicily* contains ten stories that will change the ways we view Italian life and immigration. Messina's contribution to the "verismo" school of Italian writing is unique, compelling, and bring new insights into the "miseria" of the past. Magistro's "Introduction" and "Afterword" help us better appreciate this major Italian writer.

Margaret Mazzantini
Morning Sea (London: Oneworld)
ISBN: 978-1-78074-634-0
February 2016

You might not know what it's like to be a modern immigrant to Italy, in fact you might be someone who could care less, but if you read Margaret Mazzantini's new novel you'll get closer to knowing and caring.

Morning Sea is the latest by the actress and storyteller who gave us prizewinning works like *Don't Move* and *Twice Born*, — made into a film directed by Sergio Castellitto, starring Penelope Cruz. Beautifully translated from the Italian by Ann Gagliardi, the novel tells the stories of two families who shared similar paths across the Mediterranean Sea between Sicily and Libya. Both leave homes for better lives spurred on by political and economic conditions they cannot control.

Farid, the son of Omar and Jamila, comes from a family of Bedouins who have settled in the new Libya, ruled by Colonel Gaddafi where they live peacefully until the Arab Spring of 2011. Omar refuses to join loyalist forces in their battle against his people and his widow and son must head for the sea, a place that Farid has never been. Once they arrive on the shore they are lead to an old boat carrying too many refugees. Their crossing becomes the sad story of what must be done to survive.

On the other shore, in Sicily, plays Vito on the beach, gathering what the waves bring in from out on the sea. He's the son of Angelina the Tripolina. She was born in Tripoli to parents who were among the Italian colonists of 1938; Angelina was a child when Gaddafi forced her family out with all the Italians in 1970. She suffers from "mal d'afrique" — the nostalgia of her childhood in Libya combined with the terror of having been forced to return to her parents' homeland as a refugee. While she marries and gives birth to a son, she cannot overcome being, what her husband calls her, "a deportee." Vito's father has moved to New York and remarried. While he enjoys his time in the big U.S. city, he wants to see the land that his grandparents have told him so much about.

When Angelina returns to Libya with Vito and her mother, Angelina tracks down Ali, her old boyfriend, only to find that he's living happily with several wives and loyally serving in the Colonel's Secret Police, and Vito learns why his mother has behaved so strangely all these years.

The story returns to Farid and his mother on the refugee boat that become little more than a body barge, ferrying corpses hidden by those who are afraid to let their dead loves slip into the sea.

Angelina has never liked the sea, but later as she learns to live without Vito as the boy has moved to London on his own, she wanders toward the waves and comes upon the shed where Vito kept the treasures he gathered from what floated up on the beach. Here she finds what other have lost at sea, never knowing how connected she is to the junk her son used to collect.

The power of this story is in the simplicity of its events and the compact style of writing that Mazzantini uses to carve scenes that evoke strong feelings for strangers. You might never know a refugee, but having read *Morning Sea*, you will feel what it might be like to have lived and died as one.

Melania Mazzucco

Vita (New York: Farrar, Straus and Giroux)
ISBN: 0-374-28495-4
September 2008

Melania Mazzucco is not a stranger to Italy's most prestigious literary prize. This young author was twice a finalist in the Strega contest for her previous novels, *Il bacio della Medusa* (1996) and *La camera di Baltus* 1998. In 2003 she finally won the prize for her novel *Vita*. Translated into English by Virginia Jewiss, Vita represents the best of what Italians have so far produced in terms of the literature of emigration to the United States. It has taken more than one hundred years for Italians to start paying attention to a part of their history that changed Italy and the U.S. most dramatically, and this novel could be signaling a new movement utilizing the rich and enchanting resources the U. S. immigrant experience.

Whether you like this novel or love it will depend on how much you already know about the Italian emigrant experience to the U.S. during the early 1900s. The more you know, the less you'll get out of the historical information that's presented in a rather too straightforward, encyclopedic manner, and the more you'll have to depend on the wonderfully rendered stories to get you through. The less you know about the experience, the more you will get out of both the history and story of this work, for the sensual heat of Mazzucco's prose is too often chilled to lukewarmth by the mechanically, cold public history of the immigrants she inserts, especially during the World War Two section entitled "The Road Home". Though she's weak she is weak in weaving the history of the individual into the history of a people, Mazzucco is extremely talented in rendering images and in telling compelling stories.

Mazzucco, the author, finds herself as a character in the novel as she tells the story of her grandfather Diamante's trip to Ellis Island 1903 with nine-year old Vita. Their life in New York's Mulberry Street little Italy is wonderfully depicted and takes the novel far above many of those written by Italian Americans. A young boy's romp with the Black Hand and a young girl's daring independence on the streets of Manhattan were never so alive. Mazzucco's at her best in imagining the interaction between Vita and Diamante and the many other characters who populate the scenes set in turn-of-the-century New York. She has learned that no matter how our ancestors have hidden and ignored their past it can affect our lives in ways we can only know if we explore and uncover their lives. This is perhaps the most important contribution that the author has and can make to the literature of the immigrant experience, and she does this enviably better than most.

It's hard to tell if the problem is the novelist's or the translator's, but the sometimes milquetoast metaphors, perhaps stronger in their native language, get in the way of the beautiful images Mazzucco's capable of creating—as when she is describing a young man in a too-small suit that makes him look like "the sapling at a nursery that has grown too big for the ring with its name on it". It took me a long time to read this novel for two reasons: one, I often read passages over to savor their beauty; and two, I would get bogged down in the historical prose that often interfered, separating the well-crafted images from the unraveling story. The stylistic tension between fact and fiction aside, *Vita* is an important addition to Italian American cultural history.

Clara Orban
Terra Firma (Gainesville, FL: Florida Academic Press)
ISBN 1-890357-19-7
July 2007

There is danger whenever a professor of literature publishes a work of fiction; people will act surprised, as if years of studying should preclude someone from trying her hand at that which she knows best. Fellow critics look for all the mistakes that rationalize their own fears of taking a shot at creation. Clara Orban, a specialist of early 20th century avant-garde poetry and prose in France and Italy, has taken that risk and produced an intriguing, if somewhat overwritten, first novel. A chapter from that work won a second place award for fiction in the 2003 Cassell Network of Writers/Florida Freelance Writer's Association contest that this led to novel's publication.

In many ways *Terra Firma* contains all the fury and some of the flaws that we could expect from a first attempt at book-length fiction. This family based saga of the plight of two families, one Hungarian and the other Italian, covers the familiar ground of World War II refugees and immigrants to the United States in ways that are both intricate and intimate. Her descriptions and observations make predictable scenes shine and teach us new ways of seeing some old material. It is this description that takes us deeper than the human stories presented. Orban's narrative fashions a complex background against which the simple drama plays out from the country outside of Budapest and Bologna, and into the urban centers of Europe,

The novel opens with a young woman's trip back to Italy to bury her mother. This section, called "Terra Incongita" is born out of the questions this woman has about her family's past, questions that get answered through subsequent chapters which come to us from the point of view of various family members. The last two chapters, "Roots" and "Terra Cognita," brings us back to the young woman who has learned the story of her parents' immigration only after her own long search for roots. The author's narrative skills shine best here, as the voice seems better suited for the material presented.

What's strong here is the family story; what's weak is the history that's dryly prepared and dropped in to make sure the reader understands what's going on around the families as they struggle to survive during difficult times. Could be the teacher in this writer that creates the striking contrast between the history lessons presented more like news reports and the intimate observations by any one of the narrators. The author's presence is often betrayed by a monotonous voice that seems to speak for the characters contrasting sharply to those of the characters. These problems are more distracting than destructive and keep the author unbalanced between literalness and literariness. There's a nice poetic feeling to the structure of the novel that creates an argumentative development from the unknown to the known, as the titles of the first and final chapters show. No doubt there is a poet inside this author that needs to convince the academic to give it more room.

All this is to be expected in the first novel of someone who has devoted much of her life to her studies and teaching. What makes Orban's debut fiction worth reading is that all along she never stopped paying attention to the world outside the ivy walls and used what she learned inside them to create a worthwhile work of art.

Linda Barrett Osborne and Paolo Battaglia
Explorers Emigrants Citizens: A Visual History of the Italian American Experience
(Modena, Italy: Anniversary Books)
ISBN: 978-88-96408-14-8
September 2014

For many years, the Library of Congress has been the source for much of what has been published in fact and fiction about Italian American culture. Many have been the documentary films that have used photos and texts from this great American resource. Now, a team of Italian scholars including Paolo Battaglia, Antonio Canovi and Mario Mignone, have joined Linda Barrett Osborne, former senior writer and editor from the Library of Congress, to create a visual history of the Italian American experience. The result is a selection of 500 illustrations and photos in black and white and color, set in a verbal context that attempts the near impossible task of capturing the experiences of the Italian immigrants to the U.S.A. and their descendants who we call Italian Americans.

With a Preface by James H. Billington, Librarian of Congress, a Foreword by Martin Scorsese and an Introduction by Professor Mignone, the book covers more than two centuries of history through the usual organization, as the title suggests, of such books. So the question is, what's so different about this book?

We've had Vincenza Scarpaci's *The Journey of the Italians in America*, along with many others over the years, and while they have piqued our interest in many ways, none has the breadth and beauty of this publication. The reproductions of maps, engravings, folios, historical photos, postcards, are virtually flawless. There is substantial documentation of the illustrations that provide important contexts for understanding the importance of each in place and time.

Each section is introduced by either Mignone or Canovi through general overviews that help situate the subsequent images. These introductory writings glean from the usual sources for their summaries, sources that scholars in the area know all too well. The authors have chosen to organize the text in a way that could be considered rather controversial. The Explorer section concerns the experiences of those they call Italians, those born in Italy and who explored or immigrated to the United States; the next section, Emigrants contains the experiences of those the authors call Italian Americans; and the final section, Citizens, focuses on those the authors have called American Italians. I, for one, don't get the difference, and it seems to be a rather arbitrary and possibly confusing way of separating, unnecessarily, the experiences of the immigrants, and their descendants.

All that aside, you buy this book for the incredible visual images and not for historical analysis, which is better left to the more experienced scholars of the Italian American experience. Each of the authors and introductory writers has a sense of self included in their contributions, and this makes the book more of a personal response to the experiences; it also accounts for the selections they have made in the litanies of contributions in the sciences, arts, popular culture and politics that have been included. Linda Barrett Osborne tells the story of how her family changed their name from Boccuzzi to Barrett, and how she became an "assimilated American," and yet has held on to her Italian roots long enough to recognize the need to "thank them for their strength, courage, and perseverance in seeking a new and better life for themselves and their descendants, their legacy to me."

Rather than capturing "The" Italian American experience, this book leans more towards presenting a variety of Italian

American experiences, and doesn't shy away from the warts of gangsters and terrorists who also claim the same heritage. From *Rigoletto to Rock*, Valentino to Travolta, Ping Bodie to Tommy Lasorda, popular culture is the dominant motif of the image collection. The ultimate question raised by this publication becomes, what does it mean to you to be Italian American, and how can these words and images foster or challenge that sense of identity.

Vincent Panella
Lost Hearts (Apollo's Bow Press)
ISBN: 978-1-60910-283-8
May 2011

Vincent Panella is a seasoned writer who's written a memoir and an historical novel based on the early life of Julius Caesar. His new book, *Lost Hearts*, is a series of linked stories. Like pieces of a puzzle these stories long and short come together to give us a sense of baby boomer Charlie Marino's cycle of life—as a child, teen, young- and aging adult. With grit and now without some joy, Panella renders old country and city life in telling detail that captures life yesterday and today.

The opening story, "Original Sin," takes place in Sicily and tells the story of Pietro Marino, a young boy who becomes a man when he leaves his father's corpse behind to immigrate to the United States. From there the stories focus on the lives of his successors as they live in the city and suburbs of New York. From school dances to bar rooms, neighborhoods and nursing homes, the settings are well rendered to evoke a period of American history in which families formed the basic network of social relationships.

Panella focuses on the issues that other writers tend to avoid, the miseria that binds the family to each other, fulfilling the proverb that misery loves company. Many of these stories are tough and deal with adult issues that, in the past, children were more likely to witness first-hand: abuse, infidelity, gambling, drinking, illness, disappointment, loves old and new, and fear are just a few of the issues that these stories portray. Together they remind us that the Italian American family is more than the stereotypical happy-go-lucky tribe that smiles, sings and talks with their mouths full of delicious food as they gather around the Sunday dinner table.

Many of the stories are set in taverns and bars that were Charley's father's livelihood, and deal with the pathetic lives of those who bring their personal problems to public places. Some follow Charley as he makes his way into the world outside his neighborhood trying to be an artist and individual in a world that challenges it all. Panella's stories never tie up neatly in their endings, and in this way reflect more of the realities that we all face in the course of our daily lives.

There is not a weak-link in the chain of these tales. Panella knows how to show suffering with dignity, and pity without remorse. Psychologically rich without being pedantic, these stories reach above traditional story thresholds to probe the inner workings of the minds of everyday people who struggle with learning how to survive in probable but often impossible situations.

His language comes from the Hemingway school, rendering the complications of reality in simple prose. When contemplating his father's hands in a nursing home, Charlie recalls the old man's life in miniature: "shaped like fists and heading for his face; submerged in a sink full of water soapy with disinfectant and brining up a clear beer glass in his bar; used like a garden hoe to scoop spaghetti and shit from a clogged sewer pipe in a building he'd once owned with a store rented to an Italian restaurant; at the other end of a hammer smacking through their back door glass to get inside the house after Charlie's mother had locked him out in fear."

In many ways, these stories belong to all who came of age in the 1950s and 60s, — those of us with immigrant roots, who made our own ways and now are helping our parents out as we usher grandchildren in. Whether in the old country, the old neighborhood, or the suburban oasis, readers are always at home and on edge simply because we are in the presence of a master storyteller.

Carla Pekelis
My Version of the Facts (Northwestern University Press: Chicago, IL)
ISBN: 0-8101-6087-0

The facts of this matter concern Italian Jews before and just after World War II, and Carla Pekelis' version of them is one that is rarely seen. First published in 1996 in Italian as *La mia versione dei fatti*, this memoir, flawlessly translated from the Italian by George Hochfield, will capture your attention from the first sentence and hold you until just about the end.

The late Pekelis, a holocaust survivor, immigrated to the United States with her husband and three daughters in 1941 after having escaped Italy through France, Spain, and Portugal. She was born in 1907 to an Italian Jewish family in Rome and in 1930 married a Russian Jew who had immigrated to Italy from Russia during the 1920 Bolshevik revolution.

Early on we get a good sense of what it was like to grow up in Rome as the fascist regime came to power. Pekelis's early education is the source of much security and her social engagements create a sense of how nice things could be if world politics would just leave us alone. One of the key insights Pekelis provides is that of the persecution of the privileged. Her family lived quite comfortably up until the fascist persecution of Jews in the early 1930s when her husband, a prominent jurist, was barred from teaching at the University of Florence. From there, the story takes on a frantic sense of tragedy as the Pekelis family with mother and caretaker, try to find a place where they can live without the danger of persecution.

Pekelis' style of writing and her insights into the politics of the period keeps at bay the tendency one might have to dismiss the tribulations of the wealthy. But no matter how much money they have to buy and bribe their way to safety, they are never safe, and we cannot fail to empathize with this woman's story.

The first half concerns Carla's life until her husband's death in 1947 and it is this section that is the strongest in terms of tragic and triumphant story telling. The second half intensely recounts her first ten months of widowhood, and while we are concerned about Pekelis, we get more about the politics of the period than her personal life. In this section her earlier life is recalled through her travels, and it seems as though she is going through the motions of living as she tries to divert her attention away from the sorrowful loss of her husband. It is as though her husband's death has added a filter through which much of what she is really feeling is held back. Nevertheless, there is a great deal of power in, not only this woman's story, but in her story telling ability, that makes this book worth reading.

Pekelis's attitude is what you will find most attractive. She writes with such beautiful confidence that even in her moments of great fragility, she remains sturdy. The pace of the first section is brisk and the voice feisty; the second section, she becomes more philosophical and the voice, more subdued to almost a dreamlike quality. It is this contrast that reminds us of how difficult it is for anyone to bear their entire soul to strangers, and how rewarding it is when it is done right.

Stan Pugliese, esteemed historian and professor of History at Hofstra University, provides a solid introduction that sets up the historical and political background against which Pekelis sets her life's story. Photographs and an historical timeline help to maintain a sense of how the personal becomes the historical.

Paul David Pope
The Deeds of My Fathers (New York: Rowman & Littlefield)
ISBN: 978-1-4422-0486-7
March 2011

There are no such things as royal families in the USA, but if there were, then there's not doubt that the Pope family would have been one. Generoso Pope (born Papa) emigrated from Italy, and worked his way from laborer in the sand pits of Long Island to become a power broker extraordinaire. He set his sons up in true Joseph Kennedy fashion, and while the Popes never became politicians, one of them, Gene, helped to shape the way Americans view the world that his father had helped make through his interactions with gangsters, presidents, businessmen and world leaders such as Mussolini.

The story is the stuff of mythic movies, and yet is one that is virtually unknown outside the family and a small circle of scholars. Paul David Pope, son of Gene and grandson of Generoso, has made sure that the Pope family story was told. And while you might expect a certain skewed and protected version of the truth when the stories are filtered through a family member, it seems that Paul David's defiance of old country omertà has paid off in the creation of an unbiased, unvarnished, striking portrait of his ancestors.

With an army of researchers at his command, and access to the wealth of scholarship produced by the late Philip Cannistraro, Distinguished Professor of Italian American Studies at Queens College of the City University of New York and the John D. Calandra Italian American Institute, Pope has created epic history of the roles his grandfather played in building New York city, and his father played in building the power of tabloid news through the National Enquirer.

This is a more than an immigrant rags-to-riches story, though we do get the details of Generoso's tough southern Italian upbringing through dramatic recreations based on family stories and letters. With the help of "Uncle" Frank Costello, Generoso gained a virtual monopoly of the sand and stone industry that contributed to the creation of New York City. From there, Pope, Sr. moved into the media business with the purchase of the "Il Progresso" newspaper which he used, along with his money, to maneuver political machines by representing the then strong Italian American vote to local, state and national politicians.

When Generoso confides in his son Gene that he wants him to single-handedly take over the empire that Sr. had made, Gene talks him out of it, only to be pushed out later by his brothers. Gene, now without money for the first time in his life, turns to Uncle Frank for the down-payment to buy the Enquirer, which he eventually turns into the top tabloid in the country — and in the process, turns himself into a Howard Hughes type recluse.

Paul David eventually finds his way working for his father and all seems fine until Gene dies and the paper is sold. The profit is amazing, but Paul had planned on taking over, and now, with money, but without direction, he wanders in the shadows of his fathers until he decides to reconnect with his father and grandfather through writing this book and a trip back to the old country. He takes control of himself, not through his work, but through the writing of this book. Here is a man, wounded by his privileged birth, needing a father to tell him he's a man, and without that must resort to completing the transition through his writing.

The Deeds is good story and interesting history. At times it gets bogged down in all the meticulous detail that the author accumulated through his methodical approach and the incredible wealth of available research. But overall it is a well written, thoroughly documented portrait—warts and all—of three generations of Italian American life in high places and fast lanes. Illustrated with family archival photos and documents, *The Deeds of My Fathers* is a worthwhile read and a way of reliving some of your own past through someone else's story.

Stanislao Pugliese
Bitter Spring: A Life of Ignazio Silone (New York: Farrar, Straus and Giroux)
ISBN: 978-0-374-11348-3
February 2010

Stanislao Pugliese, a professor of history at Hofstra University, has subtitled his biography of Italian writer and political activist Ignazio Silone *A Life* because the man lived many lives within his own and many of them contradict the others. Silone lived by many names; born Secondo Tranquilli, he assumed a number of aliases before settling on the name by which he became famous. A Nobel Prize nominated author, Silone is considered by many to be one of the most significant writers of the 20th century even though he never strayed far from his hometown in life nor in the literature he produced.

Born into a peasant family in Pescina, Abruzzo May 1,1900, Silone lost his father when he was young, four of his seven siblings to infant mortality and an older brother to an accident. In 1915 his mother was killed in an earthquake, and he dug out her body from the rubble with his bare hands. That left him and his younger brother Romolo to fend for themselves. Both brothers found some temporary help from their grandmother and then received the patronage of Queen Elena. They were sent to separate schools in Rome and then were assisted by Don Luigi Orione, a priest who helped orphans of the earthquake.

Both brothers became involved in anti-Fascist activities through the Communist Party. Both brothers were persecuted by the Fascist regime—Secondo, eventually fleeing to safety in Switzerland, Romolo dying from the effects of his prison mistreatment. Secondo eventually was expelled from the Communist Party and lived for a while in Switzerland where he withdrew from direct political activity, began a "private war against Fascism" in which he developed his skills as a writer.

In exile he wrote three novels that established him as a major literary voice. *Fontamara* (1933), *Bread and Wine* (1936), and *The Seed Beneath the Snow* (1941). *Fontamara* put him on the world literature map in a time when Europe was struggling with Fascism and Nazism. The world was listening and soon his works were translated into many languages. His reputation grew everywhere but Italy, where the Fascist authorities made sure he was not recognized. It wouldn't be until after the war that his work would have impact on his home country, and by then he would be invited to help establish the Italian democratic government.

In *Bitter Spring*, Puglisese attempts to create a balanced sense of the many lives of Silone. Once a Communist, always a Socialist, Silone's experiences represent the many changes that Italy faced in its transformation from monarchy to dictatorship to democracy. The balancing act becomes quite difficult at times as much of Silone's personal writings were destroyed by his wife after his death—according to his request—that leaves social and personal correspondence, government records, journalistic accounts and reviews and of course, the great body of writing Silone produced during his life, as the biographer's major sources.

The pitfalls of writing about such a major cultural figure include the possibilities of sensationalizing the writer's life and ending up with hagiography instead of biography. Pugliese's earlier experience writing the biography of Carlo Roselli has served him well and he has left no source unchecked. What he does best, besides writing clearly (and personally when necessary and appropriate), is to place Silone's life and writings under a strong light, enabling us to come to our own conclusions about the many myths and stories that have surrounded this man's life. Finding out whether he was spy for the Communists, Fascists, CIA, whether he was straight or gay, a snob or a cafone, never really matters, and Pugliese is careful to avoid the quick judgments or sensational rumors that have plagued previous accounts, and he does this all with due respect to those earlier works. What you have here is a good life story based on years of carefully documented research and very little speculation on the part of the author.

Vittoria Repetto

Not Just a Personal Ad (Toronto: Guernica Editions)
ISBN: 1-55071-244-6
September 2007

Vittoria Repetto is the vice-president of the Italian American Writer's Association and is primarily known as a performance poet. She can be seen, pretty regularly, reading her poems in bookstores and clubs around New York City. A native of the lower East Side, where most of her poems are set, Repetto stares into the city scene without blinking and tosses out powerful poetic responses that will shake you out of the way you have learned to see the world, and show you a side of life you've probably never seen before.

Recently she has gathered some of her better poems into a book entitled *Not Just a Personal Ad*. Together they make a powerful statement about the clash between old-fashioned Italianness and new world lifestyles, between an overbearing, often insensitive father and his fiery, stubborn daughter who may hide her feelings to his face, but not in her poems that come from a wide range of experiences happening in the narrow geography outlined by city streets.

Repetto's poems are deceptively simple and sometimes uneven, but they often contain unique twists that will make you turn your head, or at least think twice about her subjects. These poems become puzzles, if not at the linguistic level, then at the level of thought, and there is a simple irony at work here that is not always so obvious.

Repetto is not apologetic for anything she has done and certainly not for what she is: a passionate American woman of Italian descent who tells it like it is. In one poem she is a "granddaughter . . . pazza come un cavallo," crazy as a horse, but shows us her grandmother is just as crazy as she hitches a ride home in "a one seat bakery truck"; in another she comforts epileptic mother, watching as her father leaves the two of them to deal with her mother's fit in a subway train. The "Kodak" moments in some of these poems are rife with conflicts that tear the nostalgia out of the memory, leaving us to wonder can this really be happening and how we would deal with the resulting uncertainties.

Repetto's poems often show us that old-fashioned virtue of tough love and tough lesson teaching that happens when parents with old country upbringing try to raise their kids the same. A little girl is slapped by her mother when she complains about being thrown off a slide and "the next time around/ on the slide/the bully loses." She juxtaposes the depth of old world wisdom with new age trendiness in a beautiful image of the peasant "zuppa di pane" that fed her childhood and the "ten buck" "slice of polenta/four leaves of arugula" she finds in a glossy magazine recipe.

Many of the poems become jaunts down memory lane, while others are sensuous strides through alternative lifestyles, making this a book for mature audiences in many ways. Repetto's memories are not laced with fondness, rather they are full of the understanding that comes when you find a way to reconcile the unfairness of life, liberty and the pursuit of happiness by creating a philosophy that enables you to wake up each day and try it all again. Whether she's driving a cab, cooking a meal, or sitting in a grammar school classroom, the poet pulls no punches, and the poet's persona is someone who will not let the world go by without recognizing her, and most importantly without reckoning with her way of seeing the world.

Anthony Riccio
The Italian American Experience in New Haven (Albany, NY: SUNY Press)
ISBN: 10-0-7914-6773
March 2007

Every little Italy needs to have a book like the one Anthony Riccio created for New Haven, Connecticut. Based on more than nine years of research on his hometown area, *The Italian American Experience in New Haven* is a wonderful compilation of oral histories and original essays. Riccio, a librarian at Yale University, has become an expert in the production of oral history-based publications on little Italy. His previous work on the Italian North End neighborhood of Boston, resulted in *Portrait of an Italian-American Neighborhood* and *Boston's North End: Images and Recollections of an Italian-American Neighborhood*, similar, though less ambitious projects.

With SUNY Press, Riccio has produced a sturdy, high quality, coffee-table book, with first-rate paper enabling excellent reproductions of even the most fragile of family and archival photos that appear throughout. More than a gathering of complete oral histories, Riccio has created a chronological narrative outlining the history of Italian immigration to the New Haven area using excerpts from the many first and second generation Italian Americans he interviewed in such a way as to make the story move along.

In the "Preface," Riccio recounts his own story of accompanying his grandmother on her way to have a letter from Italy read by another "paesana". His recording of the interaction of the two old women is a vivid, dramatic moment that shows us the author has an eye for the telling moments of life. What's recorded here is more than a memory; it's a life-sign for how an entire culture works and why it needs to be preserved.

Each section opens with a brief introductory essay by the author that sets up a context for the excerpts of oral histories that follow. Those histories begin with accounts of what life in Italy was like, moves to recollections of the life on the ocean crossing ships, and the settling into New Haven neighborhoods. There's a funny anecdote story about mistaking the word corn, for "corne," the horns in Italian. From there we move to stories about becoming American citizens, going to schools, and surviving the 1918 Spanish Flu epidemic that killed more Americans than all the major wars since World War I.

Responses to the Sacco and Vanzetti trial range from the reactionary to the sympathetic, and a section on letter writing helps us see the importance placed on keeping information flowing from the old country to the new. A section on fables and proverbs creates a sense of how the oral tradition could entertain as it informed. Sections on work contain accounts of life on the farm and in the factory, including stories of how the labor movement was organized.

Riccio covers an incredible amount of history here and presents accounts of what it was like for those who returned to Italy, performances of rituals to counteract "malocchio," local feasts, societies, sports, artists, and so much more. The attention he pays to the little events in different neighborhoods, as well as the devastating catastrophes such as the Franklin Street Fire which killed 15 people, World War II in which Italians proved once and for all their loyalty to the U.S. and in which some even fought against their fathers, is the key to making a project like serve all readers.

If you grew up in Italian New Haven, then this is an historic scrapbook that should be on the coffee table in your home, and if you didn't, then this will remind you of similar lives you knew when you were growing up Italian no matter what Little Italy you called yours.

Tony Romano
If You East, You Never Die: Chicago Tales (New York: Harper Perennial)
ISBN: 978-0-06-088794-3
December 2009

By day he's a Fremd High School teacher of English and psychology—for which he's co-authored *Psychology and You*. By night, and any other time he can find, Tony Romano writes fiction. Romano has devoted his life to teaching and his career to promoting good writing. With Gary Anderson, he organizes the school's annual "Writers' Week" event that features student, faculty, and professional writers' work.

After writing for years, and winning some pretty impressive awards such as the PEN Syndicated Fiction Project (twice), and having his work produced on National Public Radio's "Sound of Writing" series, Romano seems to have hit the big-time. Last year his novel *When the World Was Young* came out to great reviews. And now his collection of stories entitled *If You Eat, You Never Die* appears with equally excellent reviews.

Some of the stories in this collection have appeared in various forms in other publications such as *Whetstone*, *Sou'wester*, *Bluff City*, and *Voices in Italian Americana* and have been nominated for Pushcart prizes. An earlier version of the manuscript was a finalist in the Associated Writing Programs' annual fiction competition. So while it's been a long time coming, there was never any doubt that Romano's time in the limelight as a writer would come.

Two dozen stories are told by and about the members of one Italian immigrant family: the Comingos, or Cummings as the mother insisted on the change when they came to America. Fabio and Lucia and their sons Michelino and Giacomo—called Jimmy, (and sometimes their spouses and children) appear in different chapters that work more like puzzle pieces that you have to put together with your own connections.

The strongest pieces come from Giacomo's point of view, especially his coming of age stories such as "Hungers" and the title story. In these stories we seem to get a great sense of the tension that's created when immigrants and their children struggle with trying to find a way into American society without losing their traditions and mutual respect.

Romano wanders more when he's working with the stories from Italy: "Confidences" and "When the Rains Come". It is as though he's not quite sure what needs to be said, and so says everything he can. While these are not as compelling as his American tales, they are necessary parts of the whole, and their inclusion is justified in "Blood Lines," the collection's finale.

We follow the evolution of the family: from the parents' courtship, the struggle for work and education, the trials of American assimilation, and the losses and gains that we all experience as we move from cradle to grave. What's particularly interesting is the sibling rivalry that occurs between Jimmy (the oldest) and Michelino. Whether he's stopping his brother from blowing off his fingers with fireworks, or complaining about his little brother's "born again Italianness", Jimmy is the first-born son we all can relate to; he'll do what he needs to fit in, to succeed, and to back away from his parents' ways. When Michelino insists on restoring the family's original name and takes his father to the courts, in "City Hall," the decision is one that Jimmy can't accept, and in a later story we get his take on the act: "what's the use, he has no sons and a vasectomy so the name won't carried on by his children".

If You Eat is strong storytelling that never suffers the nostalgia that plagues so much of Italian American writing. Romano brokers a great understanding of the Italian story in the United States using broken English (a little too stiff at times) and the great insights of a keen observer; through it all he captures the wisdom that Italian folk culture brings to modern American culture, forging the Italian American. By the time the Comingos make it to the suburbs, and into the third generation, their identities are formed, but was it all worthwhile?

When the World Was Young (New York: St. Martin's Press)
ISBN: 978-0-06-085792-9
November 2007

    A Chicago native, Tony Romano is an award winning fiction writer and teacher at Fremd High School. His writing has appeared in the *Chicago Tribune* among other prominent publications, and has been produced for National Public Radio's series "The Sound of Writing". In his first book, *When the World Was Young*, he concocts a new brew from an old country recipe that reminds us all of the humanity inside the shared emotions that transcend time, nation, and culture.

    Set in Chicago in the 1950s and 1970s, the novel centers on the family created by Agostino and Angela Peccatori who immigrate to the U.S. and begin a family. Agostino turns an old funeral parlor into a bar called "Mio Fratello" that serves as the sight for much of the action. Through the stories of the main family members, Romano hauntingly renders the results of the sins of the father and the curses of the mother as they affect their descendants who must find new ways to deal with the same old problems of life.

    Santo, the oldest son begins to physically act on his attractions and in the process picks up pieces his father leaves behind, first through one of Agostino's flirtations and then with one of his indiscretions. The son inherits his father's temptations, and attempts to right his father's wrongs. His brothers, Anthony and Alfredo are two peas in a pod and in many ways avoid the worst of what happens to the Peccatori family by developing strong lives of their own and, for a while, supporting each other through their childhood. Later life trials push the two brothers away from each other. Their sister, Victoria, is a budding young woman who wants nothing more than to get beyond the old-world constrictions placed on a teen born of immigrant parents. Through confession to a young priest she searches for a spirituality that can work and help her survive the contradictions of her life.

The tragedy of death begins with Benito, the baby and perhaps the only innocent one in this story, who contracts an illness and dies before he is two. His death affects the entire family and this is the crux of the novel's development. Through powerful dialogue, peppered with Italian dialect and Chicago slang, Romano crafts a narrative that moves well and shows us all how death can overshadow life.

Each member's story of survival serves creates the novel's narrative structure. Angela, with her sister Lupa, take off for Italy, bringing along Victoria who they believe will benefit from time in the old country. Away from the temptations of modern American life, she becomes a wiser woman. When they return, they do so with a child, Nicholas, who brings the family back together. But there is no sweet resolution to the problems presented, as the family sins become secrets that form the bases for new truths. The beauty of this novel is that it reminds us that life has ups and downs that are never neatly resolved as movies and romance stories suggest.

Romano is a strong on sensory depiction and realistically creates a world that resembles the Little Italys of Chicago's past. A minor problem of the work lies in the use of Italian, which is uneven in its accuracy, reflecting weak editing, and while those who don't know Italian won't notice, those who do will find it a little irksome. These flaws do not stop the story from developing into a wonderful mythical tale of love, live and death. This is an impressive debut novel that should help raise the standards for the Italian American presence in American literature.

Mark Rotella
Amore: The Story of Italian American Song (Brooklyn, NY: Terrace Books)
ISBN: 978-0-86547-698-1
July 2011

With *Amore*, Marc Rotella brings us the stories behind the making of some of the most popular American music of the late 1940s through the 1960s created by the children and grandchildren of Italian immigrants. All your favorites are among the forty selections that Rotella has chosen for this book. From Enrico Caruso to Tony Bennet, we get not only the tales told about the songs, but a great sense of just what went into to the making of the songs and their creators.

More than history or biography, it is life recreated — the past resurrected and connected to the present through the author's own life. Rotella brings alive the time and the neighborhoods, where the music played to working class folk who kept the tunes in their brains working their way out of urban poverty and into suburban splendor. He's read news and magazine articles, memoirs, biographies; he's listened to original recordings, radio programs, and watched hours of films and television programs, and attended live performances. He's even visited historic sites where famous concerts took place. Steeped in this rich experience, his reactions surface in clear and often clever prose that makes yesterdays matter to our lives today.

From the immigrant theater there's "Farfariello," Eduardo Migliaccio who "played on Italian and American stereotypes to help ease Italians through the hardships of assimilation." Do you remember the smooth voices of Russ Columbo or Nick Lucas? I don't, but Rotella made them matter to me as he revealed the roads they paved for the likes of Sinatra, Perry Como, Vic Damone, Al Martino, Mario Lanza and many more.

In the process of bringing their stories out, Rotella tells the story of a people who, while acculturating well, never totally assimilated into American culture. Sinatra might have never recorded a song in the Italian language like his contemporaries Jimmy Roselli, Dean Martin and Jerry Vale did., but he also refused to change his name to Satin, and stood up for the rights of his African American friends.

This book breathes, with voice and feeling. Rotella's descriptions are so on target that you can almost hear the songs through his words as in this reconstruction of the Doo Wop sound of Dion and the Belmonts: "The bass line that seems to come out of Carlo Mastrangelo's nose — 'dun dun dun, duh-dun dun-duh dun" — feels like the revving pulse of a very loud, very powerful Corvette. Then Freddie Milano, Angelo D'Aleo and Dion Di Mucci pick up the harmonization, singing in falsettos each work, "know — why — I," then all three join for "love you like I do".

Overall he does a good job of tying Italian American cultural history to the larger story of America from the 1920s through the 60s. However, when discussing an extortion attempt on Caruso he tries to connect it to the murder of the New York City police detective Joseph Petronsino, he makes an error that only helps to keep the myth alive that there was a direct connection between Black Hand activities and the origins of "Mafia" in the U.S..; while it's a common error, perpetuated by years of bad reporting, it's one that a book like this could have helped to dispel. Too bad he didn't get to Robert Lombardo's new study of the Black Hand in Chicago.

There are two chapters that do not feature Italian Americans, one on Elvis Presley and another on Sammy Davis, Jr. While these chapters do connect to the theme of the book, I would have liked to see more on some of the lesser-known Italian

Americans in music, such as Lou Christie, the Four Seasons, the Rascals and others. As they stand these two chapters on these "honorary Italians" seemed to imply the author ran out of steam along the way. However, with a little more digging, I think he would have been able to come up with more material to make the entire book a tribute to all Italian Americans in the music business.

Suze Rotolo
A Freewheelin' Time (New York: Broadway Books)
ISBN: 978-0-7679-2687-4
August 2009

If you've ever wondered who that woman was leaning on Bob Dylan's shoulder on the cover of his *Freewheelin* album you can now learn all about Suze Rotolo as she tells the story of how that cover photo was made, and many more, in her memoir about life in Greenwich Village in the 1960s.

If you're looking to get the typical gossip kiss and tell on Dylan, go elsewhere. Rotolo's too classy for that. If you're looking to get insight into how an Italian American red-diaper baby grew up, mostly on her own, and created a wonderful life out of what happened to her as she made her way through the arts scene of New York in the lively New York city neighborhood that's been home to the artistic avant-garde for generations.then you're in for quite a read.

Suze is interesting in her own write. Her prose style shows artistic originality and intelligence as she tells stories in clear language that often verges on poetry. She is an artist trained sporadically in New York and Italy. So it's not surprising that her word sketches are sometimes abstract comments on life and sometimes evolve into detailed, painted scenes. She speaks of yesterday through the wisdom of today, but never loses that sense of first excitement and fear that comes when a 17 year-old is trying to make her way in the world.

She punctuates her narrative with excerpts from journals she kept over the years, newspaper clippings, and period photographs. The result is a scrapbook of reminisces pastiched to create a sense one woman's experience growing up in '60s Greenwich Village. She writes honestly and pulls no punches:

"Secrets remain. Their traces go deep, and with all due respect I keep them with my own. The only claim I make for writing a memoir of that time is that it may not be factual, but it is true." Her goal is to "capture the emotional truth that defined the experience". And she does.

Much of who she becomes was shaped by her early family life. Her father Gioachino was an immigrant from Bagheria, Sicily who met his father in the U.S. with his mother and siblings when he was two. He became a painter and a union organizer. Her mother, Maria, was born in New York to immigrants from Pezzati in Piacenza, and after a rough childhood became an editor and columnist for the Italian American Communist newspaper "L'unita". She felt the persecution of her parents and their friends and grew up shy of Communist Dogma, but strong in her faith that justice required dedicated struggle.

Suze's done secretarial work, production work in theaters off and on Broadway, waitressed in donut shops, and pretty much whatever she needed to do to survive, support her "political beliefs based on a dislike of injustice and a fear of the bomb". She stands by convictions that while instilled by her upbringing became shaped by her own thinking and actions. Through it all she gained a good sense of the times: "The 1950s were a very repressive and politically black-and-white time; there were no shades of gray. To conform was the ideal and to be different was to be suspect". Suze goes on being different and challenging the status quo throughout these formative years.

Just as Bob Dylan alone did not make the 60s, he did not alone make a reason for Suze Rotolo to write this book. The two of them were lucky to meet each other when they did and our world is definitely better because of both of them. It would be great to get her take on the rest of her life. How about it Suze, ready for an encore?

Mark Saba
The Landscapes of Pater (Port Jefferson, NY: The Vineyard Press)
ISBN: 1-9300067-34-8
March 2005

These days, to get published by a big press you need to have a big seller, and since most big presses believe that real literary type books don't sell, they stay away from works like Mark Saba's *The Landscapes of Pater*. Now I'm not going to say that this book is a must buy, by any means. But if you like good writing about the small things in life, then you might consider picking up this novel.

Saba's a good writer who's had poetry and fiction published in many places; his epic poem, "Judith of the Lights," was part of a publication that won a 1996 Mellen Poetry Prize. *The Landscapes* is his first novel and tells the story of a young man's college daze. Saba's good at getting feelings to come alive through words. Nick Pater's father died when he was quite young and as he grows up he searches for his father in all his male relationships. Through the guys he meets he finds new ways of being himself.

Most of the story revolves around Nick's experiences in a college fraternity at a public university and his later transfer to an elite private college. There's a feeling here evoked through the kind of writing you find in works like John Knowles' *A Separate Peace*. Saba's story is moved by plot as much as it's moved by the story of a young man overcoming the shadow of his father's loss. When he travels to Sardinia, the land of his father's father, his namesake, he connects to Grandpa Nicola and is free, finally, to love the life he lives.

Paul Salsini
Dino's Story (iUniverse books)
ISBN: 978-1-4502-1080-5-2-6
November 2011

Forty-five years ago Florence suffered from its worst flood ever, damaging thousands of precious works of art, over a million books, and leaving more then twenty thousand families homeless, and forcing thousands of business to close. Paul Salsini uses that historical catastrophe in his latest work, *Dino's Story: A novel of 1960s Tuscany*. The final novel of his Tuscan trilogy, *Dino's Story* follows Dino, the son of a fallen partisan hero of World War II and a woman who's struggled to raise him properly as he grows up and out of the village that was almost destroyed during the Second World War.

If you have read Salsini's earlier books, you'll find that some of those characters have returned in this new work, and you gain the sense of the community that has contributed to shaping the worldview and values of their offspring. We follow Dino has he develops an interest in reading and the arts, and see him influenced by writers such as Alberto Moravia and neo-realism filmmakers like Vittorio DeSica. These were certainly rich times for Italian art, and through Dino, we learn how the post-war culture turned the eyes of many Italians away from destruction and toward creation.

Dino develops an interest in drawing and art and hides behind these during his youth. When he leaves his little village of Sant'Antonio takes off to study at a prestigious art school in Florence, we find him beginning to work out of his shell as he finds a place for himself in the post-war Italian art scene. Dino, who plays a pretty good guitar, does well with folk music, but when the Beatles come along, he finds that by playing their songs he can command the attention of his peers better than through his conversations. He reaches adulthood just when Florence is falling apart and plays a role it its resurrection. The drama picks up as Dino discovers someone who might be his estranged uncle, living in poverty in the city. The mystery begins as he begins to uncover the clues as to this man's identity.

Salsini realistically recreates the human struggles, sufferings and triumphs during tough times through this young man's coming-of-age. Through Dino's eyes we see the haunting hangover of post-war poverty, key treasures of Florentine art, the influences of American popular and political culture, the tragedy of a natural disaster, and the triumph of a people experienced with rebuilding their culture.

Salsini captures the changes in Dino as he moves from the relatively safe haven of Sant'Antonio to the unknown city life of Florence. For the first time he sees not only the beauty of the art world but also the poverty of the real world. "Wearing threadbare clothing and often dirty, the poor begged for food and money on the streets and in front of the churches. It was always a shock to come out of the grandeur of the basilica and find a woman crouched on the steps as she held a baby and a tin plate."

With this book he hits his stride as a novelist and leaves behind much of the journalistic technique employed his in previous books, by focusing on Dino's interior life. Salsini's research once again is impeccable and serves well to anchor this young man's story to an unforgettable place and time in Italian history.

The Cielo (iUniverse books)
ISBN: 0-595-40697-1
December 2007

Milwaukee native Paul Salsini has written his first novel based on facts and stories he heard from his cousin who survived German occupation and the Allied invasion of the region where his grandfather was born. *The Cielo: A Novel of War Time Tuscany* recreates actual events in an imagined place to deliver a story that's long on action and short on style. This veteran journalist dramatizes thorough research, showing us how World War II was a difficult and dangerous time to be a good Italian.

Tom Santopietro
The Godfather Effect: Changing Hollywood, America, and Me (New York: Thomas Dunne Books/St. Martin's Press)
ISBN: 978-1-250-00513-7
September 2012

Two score and three years ago, *The Godfather* brought forth on this continent, a new image of Italian America, conceived in one man's imagination and dedicated to the proposition that Mario Puzo needed money. With the publication of *The Godfather* in 1969, Puzo was instantly promoted to celebrity status. Not since the 1939 publication of Pietro Di Donato's *Christ in Concrete* had an American author of Italian descent been thrust into the national spotlight.

This one novel has done more to create a national consciousness of the Italian American experience than any work of fiction or nonfiction prior to or since its publication. It certainly was the first novel that Italian Americans, as a group, identified with, appearing right when Italian Americans were just beginning to emerge as an identifiable cultural and political entity. Even though this book was much more a work of fiction than any of the earlier, more autobiographical, novels written by Italian Americans, the novel created an identity crisis for Italian Americans.

This year marks the 40th anniversary of the first *Godfather* film, and writer Thomas Santopietro, a third-generation Italian American has written a book that attempts to explain the effect the films have had on American culture and his own family.

Through well intentioned but weak research, and in a lively, accessible style, Santopietro tries to explain the power that the films have had on group and personal identities. *The Godfather Effect* follows other books by successful Italian Americans who have reached a point in their lives that they feel they can safely identify with this overly misunderstood ethnic group. Here we think of the poetry of Lawrence Felinghetti, the nonfiction of Gay Talese, Diane Di Prima, and many others.

Santopietro, who has written books on celebrities such as Barbara Streisand, Doris Day, and Frank Sinatra, focuses his attention on the pre- and post-production elements of the three Godfather films, covering such aspects as the films' cinematography, set designs, music, acting and promotion. He dug through the mountains of articles and books previously published on the subject, extracting information that, combined with his personal story, make for an interesting read.

Where he is weak is in his commentary on the Italian American community. He presents observations without rigorous analysis, and his scholarly pronouncements without the necessary scholarly apparatus can be deceiving. His dependence on the only extant popular history of Italian America, *La Storia* by the late Jerre Mangione and Ben Morreale, leads him to making statements that are dated, creating for those who don't know the material, a sense of knowing something that is more complex than Santopietro suggests.

The author gets it right when he tells his own story as an assimilated grandson of Italian immigrants on his father's side, effectively contrasting their experiences to those of the WASP Americans on his mother's side. This occurs best in his chapter entitled "Patriarchy". He also tells a compelling story of the making of the films and picks up on the films' sophisticated ironies that most activists never caught. He hits the nail on the head when he writes, "For good and occasionally bad, in a manner comedic, serious, and oftentimes highly profound, *The Godfather* did nothing less than help Italianize the United States." But just what is the Italian has the U.S. become? This is a question answered by many of the books Santopietro consulted, the problem is, those answers are filtered through his own story, which, for some could be their own stories, but for most of us it does little more than make us think of how this act of culture has distorted the perception of many other Italian American contributions to U.S. culture.

Joseph Scafetta, Jr.
The True and Unbiased Story of Christopher Columbus (Fairfield, NJ: Columbia Press)
ISBN: 1-57166-379-7
May 2006

May 20th marks the 500th anniversary of the death of Christopher Columbus. And while it's hard for us today to believe that for most of those years, Columbus was forgotten and uncelebrated, he most certainly was. Columbus only began to be publicly honored in the United States when Italians started immigrating to the U.S. in great numbers. In no time, Columbus became a symbol for and of Italian immigrant whose arrival to the U.S. was anything but celebrated. It was easy for Italians to project their experiences onto an accepted hero in American history, and to celebrate their discovery of the U.S. as a way of improving their lives. Social and fraternal organizations quickly adopted the celebration of Columbus with great enthusiasm, and it wasn't long before Columbus Day became synonymous with Italian American Day. All was fine until historians started digging up the dirt.

Many look to the year 1992 as the time when Columbus's reputation was tarnished by alternative histories that started to appear. Many of what some people derogatorily refer to as "revisionist histories" began to appear and this lead to more visual and vocal protests of the U.S. celebration of Columbus. Some of these histories, accused of distorting the facts, were dismissed by Columbus defenders and embraced by Columbus attackers. In no time, attacks on Columbus were perceived by many as attacks on Italian Americans. Italian Americans, such as those in Denver, Colorado, took the Columbus Day protests personally and saw the need to defend their rights to celebrate their culture.

It was inevitable that the good and bad about Columbus would surface. As Scafetta's book points out so well, the facts on Columbus were always available, it was just a matter of whose version of the facts you chose to read. Scafetta's book unites the articles he originally published in the *Fra Noi* between October 1998 and October 2005. The author has gone through a great number of the major sources of previous histories of Columbus to take us through the seafarer's life from childhood to death. He helps us to understand the social and political situations that created both Columbus the man and the myth. His writing is deceivingly plain and simple, and the production of the book is so modest as to make you think you might not be able to take his efforts seriously. But without the prestige of a major press, nor the style of an expensive publication, Scafetta has produced a good introduction the history of this complicated figure.

Scafetta, a successful patent attorney, wanted nothing more that to present the facts on Columbus's life and leave it up to readers to make up their own minds. To his credit, and perhaps a testament to his legal training and experience, Scafetta tries to let a number of versions of the facts speak for themselves. When he does comment, it's only to point out where the controversies are and what support various interpretations might have.

To the reprints of his *Fra Noi* articles he's added a final chapter that recounts the efforts to make Columbus a saint. What the Catholic Church did not do, many Italian Americans have done. And whether you support or attack the celebration of this historic figure, Scafetta's book will help you understand how both sides of the story could be warranted. If *The True and Unbiased Story of Christopher Columbus* does take a stand, it's for making informed decisions, and Scafetta is to be applauded for presenting information that should help us all do just that.

Vincenza Scarpaci
The Journey of the Italians in America (Gretna, LA: Pelican Publishing Co.)
ISBN: 978-1589802452
June 2009

Very few scholars have tried to capture the whole of Italian American history in one book, and it seems the more one tries, the more unwieldy Italian Americana becomes. The latest attempt comes to us in a less scholarly, but interesting project by Dr. Vincenza Scarpaci.

Scarpaci, a veteran historian and teacher of courses on American and immigration history at schools such as the University of Oregon, Seton Hall and Towson State University, has spent a lifetime studying Italian American culture. In the process she's published two authored books, including *A Portrait of Italians in America*, a study of Italian immigrants in Louisiana, and numerous articles and essays in Italian and American journals and magazines.

Her latest book, *The Journey of Italians in America*, is an historical survey of Italian immigration and assimilation into North American culture told through short essays and hundreds of photographs. The process of creating *The Journey* took Scarpaci on her own travels to many Italian American public and personal archives. While the book has short essays, its strength lies in the nearly 500 photos, nearly one-third in color, that illustrate the brief writings that open each section.

Scarpaci begins with an overview of Italian immigration through chapters entitled "Origins: Life in Italy," "The Trip," "Spanning the Miles: Maintaining Ties," and "Bringing Italy to America." She then moves to "Finding a Home," "Italians at Work," "Civilizing America," and variations on the theme of becoming and being Americans that cover Italians in many areas of U.S. history. She concludes with sections that examine Italian American issues such as Christopher Columbus' legacy, crime and discrimination, the end of Little Italys, the return to Italy, and the future of Italian American heritage.

Each brief opening essay is followed by photos with extensive captions. The photos generalize the experience, while the captions work to personalize it. Scarpaci tips her hat to the many scholars and artists who have been working for the past fifty years to capture this culture before and during its assimilation into U.S. and Canadian cultures. While she covers a great deal more than most previous books, she only skims the surface of possibilities when it comes to writing Italian American histories. More than anything, this book is a testament to the diversity of Italian American experiences and should inspire others to take her cue and write more detailed and documented histories. To her credit, she acknowledges the impossibility of preserving the past in any single book. As she writes, "While we can honor the past, we cannot recreate it." And while this can't be done through history, many filmmakers and fiction writers have successfully done just that.

It is only recently that Italian American culture has taken up space in public institutions such as libraries, museums and schools. For a long time, Italian American culture's strength, Scarpaci believes has come from the family. "Italian America looks toward the family as its most successful institution… Ethnic identity is closely intertwined with family; it persevered because of family and will persist because of family." The problem is that as families grow in generations they can easily disintegrate in terms of historical memory and cultural practices, and so there is an urgent need for Italian Americans to take their place in America's cultural institutions.

Essentially what she has created is a scholarly scrapbook that reflects her take on what's important in the history of Italian America. And while it can't work as a textbook in the classroom, it could make for an interesting addition to the home library or coffee-table book collections, and a good point of departure for future projects.

Laura Schenone

The Lost Ravioli Recipes of Hoboken: A Search for Food and Family (New York: W.W. Norton)
ISBN: 978-0-393-06146-8
July 2008

It's hard to write about one's past, and it's the rare book that does it well enough to make it matter to others. Marcel Proust was drawn into his masterpiece by a sense of smell, and now we have Laura Schenone's wonderful memoir inspired by the taste of her grandmother's ravioli. The result of her attempts to master that creation leads her to a search for the original recipe is more than just a culinary mystery, it is a story of how life meaning can be made through research and how a personality can be remade in the process.

The Lost Ravioli Recipes of Hoboken: A Search for Food and Family is a joyful story of how the author rebuilds her cultural identity one recipe at a time. It is insightful without being simply celebratory. The plot, if there is one besides tracking down her the original recipe and ingredients for her family's ravioli, unfolds through a conversion she experiences as she becomes a born again Italian American.

Her opening doubts are well reflected in such insights as: "Despite the assumptions, I always knew the truth—I was not Italian. My father was Italian, but not me. There was simply not enough left by the time my generation came around. Because of intermarriage and the passing of time, I was born in the twilight of ethnicity, the barely tail end of it."

While her story is common, the writing is simply delectable and the result is quite literally a feast made of food for thought. Schenone doesn't just tell or describe what happens, she realizes truths by recreating those experiences that inspired her and in the process, captures the sensory stimulants that provoked her attention. She recalls with a brilliancy that replaces nostalgia with new knowing, doubt, with understanding, and ethnic chauvinism with a balanced sense of ethnic pride.

Some of the general history reads as though it might better fit an encyclopedia and some of the family history comes off like stiff, home movies. Most of this is in her chapter on Hoboken, but fortunately it doesn't spill out from there.

Schenone recreates family history through her search, reconnecting with long-lost relatives, awakening dormant memories and creating new relationships with distant relatives. By the time she's finished, with her search, she's found a part of herself that was always there, it just took a return to the old country to renew it. Her travel to Liguria, a few times by herself, and the last with her husband and small children, is captured in a travelogue that is informative without being sentimental or smug. Eventually, her grandparent's hometown "feels like another place inside me. It is primitive, buried in my chest or body, it is water and mountain side by side, all open and calm."

But all is not peace and love in the happy extended family. One of the points of greatest tension is in the way father daughter struggle to relate to each other, and Schenone renders this with all the honest awkwardness that we expect when confronting the truths of our pasts.

Schenone knows that recipes are not the way back to all this, but the map that helps you create experiences worth remembering. By the time you're done reading *The Lost Ravioli Recipes*, you won't know whether to put it on your library shelf or keep it in your kitchen. This is literary art as well as a map to culinary art, for she not only concocts a worthwhile and well-written story, but also all gives you the recipes, and everything you need to make them your own.

Salvatore Scibona
The End (Minneapolis, MN: Graywolf Press)
ISBN: 978-1-55597-498-5
July 2009

Salvatore Scibona might seem like the new kid on the literary block, but he's been writing for over ten years, and has published stories in places like the *Threepenny Review*, and has been republished in a Pushcart anthology of best stories. Now, his rookie novel brought him a nomination for a National Book Award, and for good reasons. The Italian American immigrant experience was never more intricately represented than in Scibona's novel, *The End*.

Ambitious in its approach and demanding of its reader's patience, the story centers on a 1953 event that occurs and unravels in the lives and minds of the inhabitants of Elephant Park, a little Italy of sorts in Cleveland, Ohio. Through slow, methodical descriptions, the author bring us deep into the lives and minds of Rocco the baker, Mrs. Marini, a type of beneficent anti-midwife who also helps girls terminate pregnancies, and a few others like Enzo Mazzone and his son Ciccio, who fill out an interesting cast of characters.

It's as if Scibona created this world and then simply recorded what happened. While the author's at work, he's never in the way, prodding us along, guiding us to "understanding". Quite the contrary, this is a novel with pages that reward lingering and invite daydreaming. I had to read this book twice, just to do this review, something that I haven't had to do for a long time. I would get so caught up in the perspective being presented that I would let go of the plot thread, and find myself wandering back as though I had lost my way. But that can be a way of life — to follow what takes your attention and forget what you were doing. "The End" prompts and rewards rereading.

The central event that takes us into private lives is the public procession of a festa through the neighborhood streets that is halted after a group of African Americans start dancing behind the marching band. Not aware of the religious nature of the music, they dance because they believe it is a party. This event, like a communal trauma, triggers a variety of responses that Scibona weaves into conflicts of abortion, war, death and personal philosophy. It's all presented in a complicated structure and intricate style that does remind us of Virginia Woolf's sophistication, Joyce's retrospection, and Bellow's determination.

Reviewers have compared him to such great authors—including Faulkner and Didion; what we have here is someone who has extracted what he needed from his lessons of the great, and is beginning to fashion his own substance and style. "The End" displays considerable writing talent that needs to be realized again and again before we can start placing his name among the greats. Certainly we can see aspects of those writers in his work. The imitation is sometimes too obvious—especially in some of his place descriptions as "Eleventh Avenue was a throng of fruit vendors, nut vendors; the armies of the retired, the lame, the blown out and wasted . . ." That can be irksome those who have studied these writers carefully. But let's face it, not many have that kind of reading pedigree anymore, so most of his influences will go undetected.

The End is a great debut for a promising writer, will frustrate those who aren't used to the modernist greats, remind those who are that writing is made out of reading, and will please all who believe that great stories are not simply told—they can be complexly written. Scibona is a writer to watch, one I believe will come up with more good writing.

Joseph Sciorra

Built by Faith Italian American Imagination and Catholic Material Culture in New York City (Knoxville, TN :The University of Tennessee Press)
ISBN: 978-1-62190-119-8
December 2016

Joseph Sciorra, one of the few scholars in the world to take this material seriously, provides masterful insights into what most people take for granted and even more ignore. His "thick descriptions" of private shrines, *presepi* — Nativity scenes, the Rosebank Grotto of Staten Island, New York, and religious processions, are all well grounded in thorough histories and journalistic accounts of these public performances of personal devotions to Catholic saints. Through his engaging style, based on the best of ethnographic methods, he presents a study that reaches beyond the academic to inform and challenge us to see and react to this Italian American material culture in new ways.

Sciorra's "Introduction" recounts the work he did over a thirty-five year period in New York City and provides a rationale for the way he has documented not only the history of these acts, but how, over the years they have been "reproduced, discarded, and reinterpreted." Chapter One, "Private Devotions in Public Places" covers the evolution of the Roman *larari* — shrines to gods found in homes, gardens and streets of ancient Rome — to their historical *le edicole* in Italy, contemporary manifestations of these can be found in "bathtub madonnas," front stoop shrines during feste, statues and yard altars that all become what Sciorra calls "Points of Encounter, Nodes for Communication," where people can meet and discuss their reactions to these public expressions of private devotions. Along with historical data and interpretative analyses, Sciorra presents interviews with builders and devotees and includes anecdotes from his encounters over the years

Chapter Two, "Imagined Places and Fragile Landscapes," covers the traditions and practice of setting up Nativity scenes, both dramatic and static, in homes and in museums from early Italian examples such as the one created by St. Francis of Assisi in 1223 to the crèche set up annually in the Metropolitan Musuem of New York. His insights help us to see how these expressions of faith interact with contemporary life: "The presepio's power is it subtle ability to embrace us in its miniaturized intimacy and conjure a reverie of entangled thoughts and meanings. The multiple narratives revealed there offer insight into our relationship to the past and the future, to the holy and the mundane, to the self and communal, and ultimately our longings and desires."

If you've ever wondered why people decorate the outside of their homes during the Christmas season, Chapter Three presents, in great mix of academic and journalistic style, not only the history of these practices, which actually originate in Northern Europe and the U.S., but also culturally critical insights as to how these practices are rooted in conceptions of social class and taste.

In Chapter Four, Sciorra provides an in-depth study of the creation and evolution of the Our Lady of Mount Carmel Grotto in Rosebank, Staten Island. Through his study of this shrine he captures the "multivocality" of a community project through interviews with and accounts of those who were present at its creation, and those who have come along to maintain this important site of religious devotion. Chapter Five covers the important aspects of religious feste processions and their relationships to multicultural geographic spaces and their populations in the city.

Each chapter is well illustrated with clearly reproduced photos and illustrations that bring to life the impact that material culture has on spiritual developments. A concluding chapter brings all the studies together to demonstrate how past and present migrations and settlements speak to and through these public representations of personal beliefs, helping us to better understand the shifting mosaic lives in New York City.

Italian Folk: Vernacular Culture in Italian-American Lives (New York: Fordham University Press)
ISBN: 978-0-8232-3266-6

The latest from the Fordham Press series, Critical Studies in Italian American Studies, edited by Nancy Carnevale and Laura Ruberto, is *Italian Folk*, a collection of eleven essays on Italian American folklore, edited with an introduction by Joseph Sciorra, the Associate Director for Academic and Cultural Programs at the John D. Calandra Italian American Institute.

Subtitled *Vernacular Culture in Italian-American Lives* this volume is a solid addition to the core of necessary and required readings in Italian American studies. More than an overview of what the book contains, Sciorra's introduction, "Listening with an Accent," helps us see why so much of what the world knows about Italian America is so little of what really goes on.

Why is food so important? What's the story with that basement kitchen? What's up with the Watts Towers, bathtub Madonnas, poetry from the oral tradition, accordion music, festas and festivals? Whatever happened to the malocchio and Italian witches? These and many more questions are raised by select group of anthropologists, folklorists, and cultural studies scholars, and they are all answered, to one degree or another, in these eleven essays.

Simone Cinotto's "Sunday Dinner? You Had to Be There: The Social Significance of Food in Italian Harlem, 1920-1940, is a substantial look at how food and the rituals surrounding its making and consumption tells us much about how it was used to maintain control within immigrant families. Cinotto insists that food culture is as much about the Americanization of the Italian immigrant as it seems to be about preserving some sort of Italian identity.

John Allan Cicala's "Cuscuszu in Detroit" weaves a cultural tale out of a family recipe and ritual meal that is a great example of the importance of reading the general through the personal. Lara Pascali's examination of the basement kitchen in North America goes a long way to reveal the reality and myths behind this strange immigrant phenomenon.

Ken Scambray's contribution brings light to two strange works of art—Baldassare Forrestiere's Underground Gardens and Simon Rodia's Watts Towers, and explains how they reflect the frustrations, hopes and accomplishments of Italians who made their way to California. Joseph J. Inguanti's take on New York metro landscapes is a technically laden, but is an information-rich look at how Italian American identities have been constructed and reflected outside their homes. The editor's own contribution, on folk artist, poet and performer, Vincenzo Ancona takes a look at how the down-to-earth poetry of one immigrant reveals a narrative thread that counteracts notions of immigrant passivity and counterattacks the notion that high culture is the only way to civilize oneself. "Valtaro Musete" is a type of according playing that comes from northern Italy, and in her essay, Marion S. Jacobson uncovers the origins of the music and how it's translocation to the United States both reflects the past and reveals the effects that music had on immigrant identities..

What does it take to be an Italian American in Reading, PA? Joan L. Saverino uses the events surrounding sacred and secular festivities to reveal how ethnic memory effects the creation of ethnic identities. In "Changing St. Gerard's Clothes," Peter Savastano looks at the connection between traditional devotion in Newark, New Jersey and the lifestyles of those who are dedicated to this patron saint from Basilicata with a focus on the role that material culture plays in the evolution of ethnic identification.

The last two essays take us places we've rarely been in the literature surrounding Italian folk culture. Luisa del Giudice uses the occasion of her brother-in-law's death to meditate on mediation of health, illness, and healing. Sabina Magliocco's "Imagining the Strega," is a good entre into the world of witchcraft Italian American style. She introduces us to the subject and the field's major publications and personalities.

Sciorra's collection creates a community of scholars who help us see the importance of what has always been there in front of our own eyes.

Illaria Serra
The Value of Worthless Lives (New York: Fordham University Press)
ISBN: 978-0-8232-2678-8
June 2008

Ilaria Serra is the author of numerous articles on the culture of Italian emigration to the United States. Her first book, *Immagini di un immaginario: L'Emigrazione Italiana negli Stati Uniti fra i due secoli (1890-1924)*, was an exciting survey of the ways Italian immigrants have been portrayed in various media. In her latest work, *The Value of Worthless Lives*, she focuses on the role autobiography has played in turning Italians into Americans. Based on her doctoral dissertation, which she completed a few years ago at Florida Atlantic University under the direction of Dr. Anthony Julian Tamburri, *The Value of Worthless Lives* sheds light on previously ignored autobiographies and provides us with new materials to examine further.

Through rigorous research she uncovered a lost treasure in the immigrant autobiographies she studies. Serra has carefully constructed a study that, while more survey than in-depth analysis, gives us a new way of looking at Italian immigration to the United States. *Worthless Lives* shows us that the immigrants were writing their own histories, even if no one else was reading them. Her exploration of these previously ignored works provides us with a new dimension of the Italian American experience, one that does not rely on heroic deeds or historic acts to become important. The works she considers covers everyday life and so, may be of more value to a greater number of people whose ancestors might have lived similar lives.

Such early dignitaries such as Giuseppe Prezzolini, unfamiliar with the writings of immigrants whose works did not make it onto his desk, pronounced an absence that Serra's study negates. She challenges misconceptions about the immigrant's ability to write his or her own story, and does so by presenting a consideration of previous studies and then by surveying over sixty examples of autobiographical writings.

Serra writes with the authority that comes from her academic background, but also with the clarity that comes from her experience as a journalist. Building on previous scholarship on autobiography in theory and practice, this section transcends earlier work and provides possibilities for future scholars to examine the autobiographies in new ways. One of her key contributions is the idea of "quiet individualism," which she invents to explain some of the minor keys in which many of her autobiographers write. In this sense, the stories emerge from those who speak softly, mostly in their mature years, about the everyday life of no one special. These are not, for the most part, braggarts, or people setting up their own lives as examples for others to emulate.

Part two consists of six chapters in which she presents brief introductions and concise summaries to each of the autobiographers she discusses. She divides them thematically into: the working-class writer, the immigrant artist, the spiritual immigrant, immigrant women, and the successful. By adding the lens of social class, to her considerations of ethnicity and gender, she helps us better see role that common people play in creating culture. One of the strengths of this study, that is the breadth of works covered, leads into one of its weaknesses. In her attempt to give attention to many writers, she never examines any of them thoroughly to explain why either their content or style kept them from being more widely published and read. These ideas, of course, are implied in the earlier section, but it would have been nice to see these surveys expanded for more serious examination.

The Value of Worthless Lives is ground-breaking and joins William Boelhower's *Immigrant Autobiography* as essential reading for anyone interested in Italian immigrant autobiography.

Ross Talarico
Sled Run (New York: Bordighera Press)
ISBN: 978-1-59954-043-6
April 2013

With *Sled Run*, Ross Talarico, an award-winning writer of non-fiction and poetry tries his hand at the novel and comes up with a splendid coming-of-age narrative that recounts the story of Rosario Tarcone. Better known as Rosey to many and "Bright Boy" to those who matter most in his life, Rosey must make decisions between good and bad, right and wrong, and what family and friends think is right for him. He's a good kid, who, like the best of good kids, knows what it's like to be bad, and isn't afraid to defy rules and commandments to do what he must to survive in a neighborhood controlled by parents, teachers, and gangsters. Mostly, he's trying to figure out how to be a man in his late adolescence, and while he believes in his father's way of living, he can't help but follow the older guys who do bad things as well as good.

Rosey is the young narrator who is trying to make sense of his Rochester, New York neighborhood. He might understand what it takes to survive, but he doesn't always get it right: "We learned one thing early-on in our neighborhood: to take action no matter how ill-advised, foolish or suicidal, and to avoid being thought of, or worse called, a coward. In the long run, it probably had to do with an integrity essential to the slim thread of manhood most of us managed to hold onto—but in the shorter run such a notion accounted for more lost teeth, broken ribs, swollen fists, and anguish than anyone might have wanted."

Talarico captures the rapture and anguish of young adolescence through Rosey and the boys of his neighborhood who grow up in the shadow of gangsters who garner their attention and often their obedience. Rosey learns that sometimes, Christmas giving and receiving requires taking. When the older ringleader, Carm Carlotta, enlists Rosey in the annual sled run—the name for a ritual through which mob leaders take from community businesses to give to those in need—Rosey learns what a future as a hood could be. But Rosey's no simple character; when a poem he steals from his father's notebooks winds up on the front page of the local paper, he learns what family, life, and death are all about by confronting his father's feelings. Rosey, unlike others, learns to negotiate between two very different models of manhood to give us a sense that someday he just might do some good in the world.

Talarico, in elegant simplicity weaves a tall tale that rivals some of the best Christmas stories in the English language; this one takes place in a little Italy that has problems with outsiders, and solutions all too reminiscent of racist incidents of the past. This is gritty storytelling that yanks truths out of pain and love out of mistaken acts. Central to Rosey's life are his friendships with Danny (whose father hates Rosey), and Cosmo; the three of them form an alliance that rivals the Three Musketeers. From foolish acts like dancing in a fire into which bullets have been thrown, and pranks involving dead rats, to outright illegalities, the trio forms a bond that is stronger than family and the very forces that lead them astray.

Sled Run is a tight story that glides cleanly from a peak of a magical realist preface through a traditional realist plot, and comes to a comfortable stop right in the middle of a new American Christmas myth. Talarico's prose never draws attention to itself. This is pure story, through and through, one that you can read over and over again, and one that calls for attention to filmmakers looking for a new angle on an old theme.

Aldo Tambellini and Arturo Giovanitti
Parole e sangue (Isernia, Italy: Cosmo Iannone Editore)
ISBN: 9788851600600
12 Poems www.voicesinwartime.org
April 2006

Radical poets: then and now

The spirit of Italian American radicalism may be more in the past than the present, but you wouldn't know it from two recent publications. First, there's a great collection of the poetry of the late, great Arturo Giovannitti, and then the first collection of poetry from celebrated video art pioneer Aldo Tambellini. Both publications tell us that the voice crying out against injustice is as poetic as ever.

For those who know Giovannitti, this is a must buy publication. For those who don't know one of Italian America's poetic masters, this is the best way to get to know the man who helped led the famous Lawrence Strike of 1912. Giovannitti, born in Ripaborroni in Molise, Italy in 1884 and died in the Bronx in 1959. At the age of 17 Giovannitti immigrated to North America and lived in Montreal, where he studied theology at McGill University, and then moved to the U.S. He worked with the Industrial Workers of the World and with the Italian Socialist Federation. More than a union activist, Giovannitti was a staunch anti-fascist who also published his poetry in all the major left-wing periodicals of his time including *The Masses*, Carlo Tresca's *Il Martello*, and many others.

Scholar Martino Marazzi, who gave us *Voices of Italian America* and *Misteri di Little Italy*, has compiled the important poems of Giovannitti's collections *Arrows in the Gale* (1914), *Quando Canta il Gallo* (When the Cock Crows), first published in Italian in Chicago in 1957 and *The Collected Poems* from

1962. Once again Marazzi has done brilliant detective work in tracking down the publications and annotating the edition with an excellent overview of the value of Giovannitti's work, a brief biography and a note on the edition. An extra plus is the inclusion of two great essays by poet Joseph Tusiani who saw Giovannitti as a mentor and friend.

Most of what appears here is in Italian, and if you read Italian you will be pleased to have so much Giovannitti in one place. About a third of the publication contains bilingual versions of the poems. This is important as Giovannitti did write in both English and Italian and never before have these poems appeared together.

What's most characteristic about Giovannitti's poetry is how he sanctifies the everyday life and actions of the workers through his own life. A man who lived for justice, GIovannitti put his body where his words were and his words were other's bodies could not go. He is, in many respects, one of Italian America's most valuable resources, and thanks to Marazzi, we can now get to know this master once again.

While Aldo Tambellini may never reach the heights of Giovannitti, he is nonetheless committed to calling our attention to the contemporary injustices that plague our society. There is no doubt that Tambellini is writing about the very things that Giovannitti would had he still been around to see things like the Iraq War.

Tambellini, as Anna Salamone tells us in the introduction to his first book of poems, is a survivor of World War II who knows the horrors of war, having lived through the January 6, 1944 bombing of his neighborhood that killed 21 of his neighbors. Since then Tambellini has devoted his artistic skills to trying to stop all the wars that have surfaced in his lifetime. From Korea, to Viet Nam to the Gulf and now the Iraq war, Tambellini has led demonstrations on the streets and in theaters. The founder of the New York's famous "Gate Theater," the home of many avant-garde presentations and performances, Tambellini has turned to publishing and *12 poems* is a powerful testament to life and through 12 raw and rough poems, he reminds us of the beauty that war destroys.

Anthony Julian Tamburri
Re-Viewing Italian Americana (New York: Bordighera Press)
ISBN: 978-1-59954-020-7
July 2012

Anthony Julian Tamburri is the Dean of the John D. Calandra Italian American Institute (Queens College, CUNY) and Professor of Italian and Comparative Literature. His publications have been in the fields of Italian and Italian/American studies. The author of more than a dozen books and over one hundred essays, Tamburri has also edited more than thirty volumes and special issues of journals. Beyond this work he has contributed significantly to the development of Italian American culture through his regular blogs on i-italy.org and the Calandra Institute's television program *Italics*. All this work has made Tamburri one of the leading public intellectuals of Italian Americana.

His latest book, *Re-Viewing Italian Americana: Generalities and Specificities on Cinema*, is a virtual primer in the history and analysis of the Italian American presence in U.S. film, video and television. Written with the general reader in mind, Tamburri takes us through a thorough survey of the critical work that has been done on the interpretation of Italian American films and videos, making the case that only by responding thoughtfully to what it is that is produced can we develop an awareness of what is happening to Italian American identity.

Tamburri, builds his arguments on strong theoretical foundations, and from there moves into clear and logically sound pronouncements that reach beyond the academy into the streets where popular culture is presented and consumed. Anyone who claims to be an advocate of accurate representations of

Italian Americans needs to read the five essays and concluding thoughts in this book.

Dean Tamburri begins his book with guiding questions that outline ways of thinking about representation that enable us to better analyze the impact of stereotypes on the development of Italian American identities past, present and future. In the book's first section, "Italian Americans and the Media: Cinema, Video, Television," he comments on a wide range of what's been produced and reminds us of what has not been and what should be produced. In this historical survey, Tamburri lays out a plan for more rigorous investigation into the cultural representation of Italians in the United States from the earliest silent films to the latest reality television shows.

From here the author moves into four case studies. In the first, he revisits the public persona of Frank Sinatra through a close reading of Sinatra's Academy Award winning short film, "The House I Live In," reminding us that Sinatra held strong critical opinions of race and social relations upon which he acted, promoting a more liberal agenda than many might connect to his legacy. In "Michael Corleone's Tie," Tamburri shows us how something as seemingly insignificant as what tie the character wears throughout the film can be filled with meaning that counters much of the criticism Coppola has taken for his creation of the film.

"Old World vs. New: Opposites Attract" is the more technical of all the essays, but worth the reader's work, as Tamburri takes us through a unique reading of the film, *Nuovo Mondo* (*The Golden Door* in the English version) that helps us better understand Italian notions of emigration from Italy. And his final essay on short films establishes him as the go-to authority when it comes to this neglected genre of film art.

His conclusions will challenge to you know your history and act on the forces that created your very identity. *Re-Viewing Italian Americana* offers a thorough analysis of the current state of Italian American media representation, one that demands attention for its keen insights into how we have viewed our past, and one that offers us ways of rethinking how future identities will be formed and reformed.

Maria Terrone

American Gothic, Take 2 (Georgetown, KY: Finishing Line Press)
ISBN: 978-1-59924-426-6
July 2011

Life can be strange at times, but through the poetry of Maria Terrone, you can become more familiar with some of that strangeness and realize that it's not what happens, but what you make of it that really matters. In her latest chapbook, *American Gothic, Take 2*, Terrone takes her considerable literary talent in new directions through two-dozen poems, all of which challenge the way we live our everyday lives, showing us how to see it all from angles strange and to re-see it through words.

Gioia Timpanelli
What Makes a Child Lucky (New York: W.W. Norton)
ISBN: 978-0-393-06702-6
September 2009

Gioia Timpanelli might be called the "Dean of American Storytelling," but I like to think of her as the *Commare* of the word. Like a wise friend, her stories and writings counsel as they console, invigorate as they entertain, and unite us all with narrative threads that bind us to ancient truths. Like a midwife, her labor with words assists in the birth of new thinking about old things.

Timpanelli has won many awards for her storytelling in television and literature; her last novel *Sometimes the Soul: Two Novellas of Sicily*, won a 1999 American Book Award. Her new novel, *What Makes a Child Lucky*, brings us to her beloved Sicily, origins of much of her art, and many of the great stories of Western civilization. Based on a Sicilian folktale of a boy who is sent by his brothers to steal an ogre's treasure, *What Makes a Child Lucky?* takes off from this familiar tale and moves in new and interesting directions that renew the story for today's world.

It doesn't take a village to raise a child if you've got one good godmother, and that's what thirteen-year old Joseph finds after he is betrayed by jealous brothers who send him to the mayor's office one day. The mayor forces him on an errand into the hills to deal with some the very bandits who killed Joseph's best friend, Pasquale the wine carrier. Joseph knows his terrain well from finding food for his mother's cooking, but he has no idea what he's about to encounter when he meets an ancient woman and the bandits she cares for.

Joseph's experiences away from home are clarified one day as he listens to a shepherd piping a song: "As a child I had lived inside my own life with whatever I had found there, so I never imagined life as separate from my family, but now I saw and heard something new, something greater than my small life, something that had been created." Joseph discovers the power that comes from creating and it leads him to live a life against destruction and for art. He finds that his stories have power that he never could have imagined; they can make him visible or invisible, and through the strange experiences, mediated by Immaculata, the woman who cooks for the bandits, he learns how to prepare meals with what he finds around himself and how to live in the balance of good and evil.

It's not just Immaculata's words that teach Joseph how to handle things; it's sometimes just the way she looks at him, as when he leaves her to live with the bandits. As he turns to wave goodbye he sees that her first look is one of indifference, "Then her face changed, and without hesitation she looked right into my eyes with the most compassionate, the most compassionate look I have ever seen in my life . . . Before this moment I had only understood that word 'compassion' in terms of deeds and actions. Deeds and actions I understood; but a 'look' that could change you?"

Creativity and compassion are just a few of the lessons learned by Joseph in this tale of adventure and maturity. Timpanelli adapts her verbal art to meet the needs of the page and rewards the eye with rich imagery and the soul with strong sentiment. Often what she writes is pure music, and the songs she creates invite us to sing along. She maintains a sense of presence that is key to the oral tradition, and is able to meet the demands of the written word. This master storyteller has concocted a strange brew out of familiar ingredients. *What Makes a Child Lucky* deserves a place on every family's bookshelf. Brava maestra Timpanelli!

Joseph Torra
They Say (Niantic, CT: Quale Press)
ISBN: 978-0-9792999-0-2
December 2008

After I read Joseph Torra's novel, *they say*, I wondered what else this talented writer had produced. His first novel, *Gas Station*, was named a *Publishers Weekly* Best Book of the Year in 1996, and since then he's published three novels, six books of poetry and a memoir—quite a body of work for someone to never be noticed by Italian American critics. It could be Torra's not well known because he labors in experimental modes that have kept his work in small presses. But that should change.

In this work Torra plays with the way people speak to create a dynamic way of telling a story. You know what "they" say, don't you? "They" usually "say" something about the way things are supposed to be as in, "Well they say it's not good to leave a window open when you sleep. An ill wind might blow in," and "They say there's going to be a recession." Who they are and why they get to tell us how things should be done is hardly ever discussed. What matters is that the social authority behind the shadowy "they" forms a sounding board against which we toss our more outrageous thoughts.

Torra's "they" are the brothers and sisters of one Louis Pelligrino, who is an artist gone "pazzo" in early 20th century Massachusetts. Louie's pathetic, often tragic, life is formed by an abusive father, an elusive mother, and a society that that doesn't know how to extract the artist's talent from his temperament. Here is an immigrant saga from a very different perspective. The Pelligrinos are not the usual lovely, honorable happy urban family whose trials and tribulations in poverty are overcome to lead them all to the promised land of the suburbs and middle class bliss.

Torra's writing has a freshness that's rare in today's world of fiction. He's not afraid to take chances or to make his reader work. You have to get used to reading "they say" and it takes more than just a few pages. First of all, "they" are all the brothers and sisters of Louie who's trapped in a working-class immigrant family that can handle his talent but not his eccentricities. Secondly, most of them speak in a vocabulary and style that has not left elementary school, and so you find yourself mouthing the words out loud in order to follow the normal non-sequiturs that happen when people speak. Only when we get to Louie's perspective is there any sense of standard English, and it seems strange because according to all the others Louie is the one who's crazy.

There are no chapters and you have to pay close attention when one voice begins and an other ends. There are very subtle differences among the siblings and sometimes you have no idea who is talking. But really, it doesn't matter, as brothers and sisters all form that nebulous "they" who hover above Louie and his inability to realize his artistic talents.

Each of the ten Pelligrino kids (there were twelve, but two died young), weighs in on the events that follow their tyrant father, their traumatized mother, and the strange dynamics of this normal, dysfunctional family as they struggle to survive through The Depression, World War II, and their own extended family history. While the father is willing to help his oldest son through art school, which is more than he considers for his other children, his unchecked drinking splits the family into many pieces that find any number of ways of coming together to help, and sometimes hurt, each other.

This novel should be the one to bring Torra the attention his art deserves.

Adriana Trigiani

The Supreme Macaroni Company (New York: Harper Collins)
ISBN: 978-0-06-231416-1
January 2014

Once upon a time Valentina was a happy shoe designer, enjoying the single life—though we could all tell she was getting a little too lonely. Enter a handsome leather tanner Ginaluca Vecchiarelli, the older man from Italy who proposes to Valentina on Christmas Eve, and the rest is story.

In *The Supreme Macaroni Company*, the latest in Adriana Trigiani's Valentina series of fiction (which began with *Lucia, Lucia*, and moved through *Brava Valentina* and *Very Valentine*), Valentina seems to be skipping her way on the road to joy and self-fulfillment.

She's rescued the family shoe business, made it thrive, and is now turning attention to her personal life; but personal is not something she can keep to herself. From her hands-on mother, her proud papa, to her siblings, cousins and business associates, Valentina's life is an open book interpreted by them all, many of whom do it with a nosiness and humor that seem to be family traits.

From the opening to closing Feast of the Seven Fishes, the typical Italian American celebration of Christmas Eve, Valentina and Gianluca take a relationship ride in and out of certainty about their marriage. Things fall apart soon after the storybook wedding at Leonard's. After the honeymoon in New Orleans, Gianluca reveals news he's been hiding from her: her Argentine cousin is selling the shoe factory that manufactures Valentine's line of shoes. When Valentina finds out, she begins to question just what she's done by marrying this man. She quickly turns away from the relationship to focus on solving the resulting business problems.

Enter Mama and Papa, and the whole family, who help her discover an old, abandoned macaroni factory out in Youngstown, Ohio, where the family has some history, and everyone takes part in putting the shoe business back on track. In many ways, this experience takes them back to the roots of the family's immigrant history, and becomes a way of renewing their sense of Italian American identity and strengthening their family ties.

The key to Trigiani's literary charm is the way she integrates description with themes in the story. From the very opening, we see New York City from a distinctly female point-of-view: "The Hudson River lay flat and black like a lost evening glove," and "The big Christmas moon appeared out of nowhere, like the diamond on my hand," these and many more descriptive phrases are crafted organically so that they foreshadow future actions and allude to past events.

The novel's tension is derived from the clash of Italian and Italian American cultures, and nowhere does this appear more humorously than when she is describing the banquet hall where the reception is to be held. The major difference between Italy and the U.S. lies in the comparison of the cultures' attitudes toward their histories. Leonard's of Great Neck, New York is a pretty famous location for hosting major lifetime events. Unlike the Italian style that it copies, Leonard's lacks authenticity. "There is no history, just the dazzling patina of the stucco that resembles white teeth. Even the tiered fountain looks as though it has been dipped in Polident." If you don't get the take on Italian American kitsch here, and laugh, you're living in a dream world.

If you're looking for a fairytale happily ever after finale, look elsewhere. You should know by now, if you're a seasoned reader of Trigiani's fiction, that plot is not the center of her stories—life is, and the ups and downs in this extended family saga are what make her novels worth the read. It's not what happens to Valentina, but how it happens: how she and all the others react that make it resonate reality to readers.

The Shoemaker's Wife (New York: Harper Collins)
ISBN: 978-0061257100
January 2013

In her latest novel, Adriana Trigiani plies her master storytelling trade, one that makes bestsellers of most of her books, to an immigrant saga based on her grandparents' love story. Ciro and Enza, friends from an Alpine village in Italy, struggle to make their lives matter in a world torn by war and abuse in the church and workplace. Both protagonists have tough childhoods that push them into the workforce while most children are busy learning their ABCs and playing make-believe.

Ciro and his brother Eduardo are left at a convent just after their father has died in a Minnesota mining disaster. Their mother knows she can't take care of them in the state she's in, and that she needs help herself. Enza's father happens to be the one driving the carriage that brings the boys to the convent and their mother to a refuge further away. Ciro grows up to be a strong, handsome young man who has been shaped by the nuns into a hard working man who is tough enough to stand up to the local church authorities when he witnesses abuse. His punishment for telling the truth is to be sent to a work farm, a sentence the sisters help him avoid by sending him off to the United States.

Enza is the oldest daughter in a family of hard working parents who can dress and guide her father's horse team as well as she can make clothes and embroider linens. When tragedy befalls the family, Enza remains strong and leaves with her father for the U.S. so that they can make the money they need to buy the land they've been renting. Their plans for a short stint in America are thwarted by hard times, but their dream is not lost. Her father works in mines while Enza finds employment in a garment factory. Her friendship to a young Irish immigrant proves to be her salvation and the two of them end up working in the costume shop of the very New York opera company that employs the great Enrico Caruso. The experiences in New York transform Enza into a strong woman.

Ciro and Enza cross paths a number of times before they connect to build a life and love together. It all happens after Ciro serves his new country in the Great War and returns to the shoemaking business that he had helped to develop into a highly profitable trade. Together with a friend he had met on his ocean crossing, Ciro brings his skills out to Minnesota to provide boots for miners in Minnesota, the very place where his father was killed.

Trigiani weaves a plot that, while predictable, remains interesting because of her ability to create characters that you can care about. Enza's experiences in the world of opera and Ciro's in the shoemaking trade remind us of what many of our ancestors went through as they became Americans. On their way, they hang on to their Italian values of hard work, the importance of family and the need for good friendships, while they take advantage of the opportunities the new world brings them. This combination is what makes their success all the more remarkable, and their tragedies, all the more heartfelt. In many ways, this is the kind of story that, while sticking close to historical facts, becomes mythic, and thus more powerful, in the hands of a skilled writer.

The addition of family photos at the end—the ones that Trigiani kept around for inspiration as she wrote—make this novel more personal than usual. There are even some discussion questions at the end for those who might want to connect the reading to their own lives. All in all, *The Shoemaker's Wife* is a good reason to stick with Trigiani as she writes her Italian ways into American culture.

Very Valentine (New York: Harper Collins)
ISBN: 978-0-06-125705-6
May 2009

The Italians call the novel "il romanzo," and to translate it as "romance" does a disservice to much fiction but not to that of bestselling author Adriana Trigiani. Her romantic takes on life Italian American style, whether in West Virginia or Manhattan, are all filled with fairy-tale like stories rooted in everyday life. She gives her readers, women and men alike, something to keep their minds off their own lives for a while; it's no wonder she fills bookstores with adoring fans. With seven bestsellers under her belt, Trigiani is one of the few active ports in the tough economic seas that the publishing industry has been facing since long before this recession.

Her latest novel, *Very Valentine*, features a likable, if not loveable, Valentina Roncalli, who in her early thirties has had enough of hearing that she should be married; while she never gets enough attention from the men she's fallen for, she gets plenty from those who've fallen for her. Valentine has a sense of humor that should have gotten her at least a "Comedy Central" special, but she is an artist, one who doesn't drift far from her

New York city roots in her attempt to make something of herself as she takes over her grandparents' shoe shop.

Valentina aches to find a balance between being American and Italian. She's Italian when she says things like, "I live for my work, I don't work to live," but the American comes out in the wash: "We're typical overextended, overworked Americans with the worst kind of tunnel vision. We waste the present for some perfect future we believe will be waiting for us when we get there?" The solution is to find, if not perfection, then at least satisfaction, in the present, and she learns this only when she travels to Italy. After a romantic disappointment, she finds herself working for a master cobbler who helps her realize the design of her dreams.

All of the action takes place in New York City and Italy, and Trigiani does a great job of setting scenes without letting them distract from the action. Much of what happens is full of the frilly details of fashion, makeup, and footwear—all things that most men turn away from when they are dragged along on a woman's shopping safari.

Trigiani uses the Roncalli family to show how the dying notion of family in the U.S. is still alive in Italy. In Italy, "the dreams of the family become our dreams," says one of her characters. Valentina responds: "I think about my family, and how that used to be true for us. It was family first, but now, it seems, my generation has let go of all that."

The author deftly balances the demands of drama to entertain and history to inform. We get history without the lessons, and the drama without the forced-hand we see so often in much Italian American based writing. Trigiani could turn any subject into a novel, mostly because she 1. Knows how to talk, and 2. Knows how to listen to her characters. Each character keeps his/her own voice and so there's never any confusion.

When everything's so smoothly executed, the smallest wrinkle stands out, so when you see "Que Bella" (along with a few other language mistakes), you wonder if the AP exam in Italian might be just what editorial houses need to insure editors get the language right.

Most everything falls into place in this Cinderella offshoot, and so it's easy to see how Trigiani style of romance will make for some good Hollywood films; one's in production right now starring Ashley Judd.

Anthony Valerio
The Little Sailor (New York: Bordighera Press)
ISBN: 1-884419-94-1
March 2009

Is it a novel? A memoir? A book-length prose poem? Actually, Anthony Valerio's latest book is a little bit of all three and a whole lot more. You might know him as the author of two books of short essays, (*The Mediterranean Runs Through Brooklyn and Valentino and the Great Italians*), a novel (*Lefty and the Button Men*), two biographies (*A. Bart Giamatti and Anita Garibaldi*) and a memoir (*Toni Cade Bambara's One Sicilian Night*). His new book, *The Little Sailor*, reveals skills he's honed to perfection through his previous work.

It's not what happens in *Little Sailor* that matters—for much of it could have, and probably has happened to many of us: we've all had childhood desires, crushes and adult fantasies. What's unique about this work is how this master storyteller concocts and serves the prose that works literary magic. This is nothing short of what I can only describe as gourmet writing. That's how carefully this writer chooses his words. "The pleasure you'll extract from this writing comes from savoring lean sentences that hold the weight of paragraphs such as: In the late afternoon, amid gulls and marsh smells of sea salt and clams and crabs, the most beautiful woman the Little Sailor's father had ever seen walks along Shelter Island's Silver Beach." It all results in images that will remain with you like powerful photographs—an avocation Valerio took up not too long ago.

Little Sailor is divided into two parts. The first, reads more like a traditional memoir, only Valerio presents his younger self as a character in the story of his past, and from this distance, anything can happen. Part One traces the evolution of the female presence in Antonio's life. The first section is entitled Brooklyn and focuses on the women of his past: friends of his mother, girl playmates, fawning aunts and strangers, and early lovers. The second section, "Italy," presents more recent life experiences in Italy where he travels with his professor wife and meditates on Italian history, art and currency. Part Two, playfully entitled "& Beyond," with two sections ("Missing Persons" and "The Bensonhurst Pigeon") is a fantasy of sorts that involves young Antonio who witnesses what could be a real-life make over of *The Maltese Falcon*; in many ways it becomes a projection of the author's dreams and nightmares and echoes ideas and actions of Part One. Cleverly punctuating the sections are interesting photographs taken by Valerio that enhance the reading experience.

In the end, we're not quite sure how to categorize the writing for if it is really a memoir, as the book's back cover suggests, then what are we to make of the appearances of a Fat Man, ex-cop, a Baronessa, Bridget O'Shaunessey, Sam Spade and their search for the real *Maltese Falcon*. We can only imagine that these are extensions of the people in Antonio's life — self-projections that happen in an extended fiction realized only in the author's mind shaped by such cinematic influences of his past. Whatever you call it, *Little Sailor* is entertaining from start to finish and holds up after several readings that its 81 pages invite and rewards.

If you'd rather have the book to read to you, while your driving to work, walking down the road, or just plugged into your I-pod, you can order the book in a compact disc version that is narrated by Valerio himself. Produced by Daisy H Productions, the oral version is a rich compliment to the book and available through Amazon.com for $24. I have both and encourage you to do the same. On the page, Valerio's prose is worth lingering over; on the cd, you get a sense of timbre and excitement that is unlike anything a book could provide. Either way or both, *Little Sailor* is writing worth your while.

James Vescovi
Eat Now; Talk Later: 52 True Tales of Family, Feasting and the American Dream
    (Author House)
ISBN: 978-1-4918-3148-9
April 2014

James Vescovi's *Eat Now; Talk Later: 52 True Tales of Family, Feasting and the American Dream* reach far beyond the Vescovi family to touch the most distant reader. Vescovi, a writer by trade, captures stories that he has heard from his father and grandparents, in a simple language that makes reading these short stories a joyful and worthwhile experience.

His father, Selvi, is an only child who has become successful via corporate America. Selvi often finds himself trapped in and frustrated by the role of caretaker, especially as his parents reach their senior years. James, the grandson, ever observant, turns his father's frustration into moving stories that capture more than family history. The way each communicate to the stories' protagonists makes for a wonderful study in the evolution of Italian identity in the United States, especially when James gives his children Italian names that upset his grandparents.

Vescovi organizes the short episodes into five sections. "La Sagra," the Feast, focuses on the food that brought this family to the sites where these stories are passed on to future generations. "Stati Uniti," covers the immigrant experiences of Tony and Desolina as they make their way from Casaselvatica, Italy to the Hell's Kitchen neighborhood of Manhattan and Astoria in Queens, New York. "Semplicita'," focuses on the simple lives led by these immigrants as they forged new identities as Italian Americans. Vescovi admits that his grandparents did nothing "grand" with their lives, other than live them honestly and full of love for their family. The way they handled their money, how they watched wrestling on television, in other words, the way they lived normally, is extraordinarily told.

"Si Ricordiamo," covers the tales recounted by Tony and Desolina of the land they left behind. Key here are the stories of the returns to Italy by Vescovi and his bride as they spend part of their honeymoon in the ancestral towns of Casaselvatica and Casalasagna where they find a key symbol of their past in a nickel-plated scythe that they bring home to hang on the wall of their grandparents' home. One generation's work has become art to subsequent generations and a way of preserving the family's history and dignity that comes from hard work. The collection concludes with "Stare per Finire," as the grandparents complete their lives, leaving a legacy of lessons for future generations.

Concluding with a few recipes and a scrapbook of family photos, "Eat Now; Talk Later," will remind you of your grandparents, even if they weren't Italian immigrants. You can sample Vescovi's literary fare and hear the author talk about his work at: http://www.eatnowtalklater.com

James Vescovi's non-fiction and fiction have appeared in the *New York Times*, *Creative Nonfiction*, the *New York Observer*, *Georgetown Review*, *Ancestry Magazine*, *Alimentum*, *The Mars Hill Review*, *Midwestern Gothic*, *Natural Bridge,* and other publications. He is author of *The USS Essex and the Birth of the American Navy* (Adams, 1999), a history of a 19th-century warship.

Richard Vetere

The Writers' Afterlife (New York: Three Rooms Press)
ISBN: 978-09884008872013
March 2014

You might know Richard Vetere through his poetry, his plays, his films, or his novels, but no matter the venue, he's a true storyteller, able to take you into a world that's familiar, but always doing it in unfamiliar ways. This is the mark of a master. His latest effort is a novel that brings life out of death to tell a story that's one of his best.

The Writers' Afterlife tells the story of Tom Chillo, novelist, screenwriter, playwright and poet who dies before he can achieve the fame of which he has always dreamed. Chillo forsakes most of what us mortals dawdle in on our ways to the end of the road; he steadfastly dedicates his time and energies to his writing, avoiding all that might take his eye off the written page. Along the way he achieves success, but not in the way he needs in order to make it into the same afterlife as those greats he studied and emulated throughout his life.

Dying at the age of 44 from a stroke, Chillo is carried dreamlike into an afterlife reserved only for artists. Guided by Joe, a minor artist from history, Chillo is taken first on a tour of the writers' afterlife where he rubs shoulders with the likes of "Eternals" such as Jane Austen, William Shakespeare, Emily Dickinson, Frank Kafka, Eugene O'Neil, Charles Bukowski and John Fante, and many more who reside in a place for those who actually achieved fame during their lives or long after their deaths because some living person persisted on the writer's behalf.

Those who don't make it to the place reserved for the Eternals go either to the place for those who were famous on

Earth but now forgotten or to The Valley of Those on the Verge, where Chillo finds himself. Joe explains that Tom will live without pain except for, "An acute sense of anxiety [for] never being famous." But there's hope even here; Tom has earned one chance to alter his state: "one opportunity to go back to life and do all you can to change the fate of your fame," and this becomes the driving force of the novel's plot.

The dead writers are able to fashion their afterlives out of the same imagination that wrought the works that made them artists. They can choose to experience all this during their favorite time of their lives, even living with their characters if they so choose.

Vetere uses the early part of the novel to comment on the status of Chillo's favorite writers and achieves a remarkable commentary on the state of literature in the mind of a writer, reminding us that literature is made out of other literature, and that every writer is, in many ways, in some type of competition with all the other writers who ever existed for an audience. He does all this in prose that's lean, direct, and keeps the wheels of plot turning to a surprising finale.

Chillo meets other promising writers in the Valley of Those on The Verge, and shares stories and sometimes bodies with those in whom he confides. He feels real love for the first time in this afterlife, and because of it, gets caught up in glitch that could ruin his one final chance to be called to his place with the Eternals. What happens when he comes back to Earth comes to us in a film-like tragi-comedy that is part Dickens, part Poe, and part Mel Brooks, but a tale that ends up all Vetere. This is what the good writers do; they learn from their predecessors, and then as they work on their craft they move from imitation to innovation as develop their skills.

Robert Viscusi
Ellis Island, the Epic (New York: Bordighera Press)
ISBN: 978-1-59954-033-7
July 2013

It used to be that the world's great epics were the foundation of a solid education: Homer, Virgil, Dante, Shakespeare, Pope, Milton were all authors whose work an educated person was expected to know well. But these days, who reads them, and better yet, who would bother writing one? While the fate of the epic seems to have been relegated to rare and formal study, one Italian American has taken on the task to create one out of the Italian American experience.

Robert Viscusi, award winning novelist, essayist, critic, professor and poet has produced a book-length poem entitled *Ellis Island* that challenges us to revisit Italian immigration to the United States and to rethink what it means to be Italian American.

Like most epics, there are heroes. But in *Ellis Island*, they are not warriors though sometimes Viscusi's heroes are certainly at war with the cultural forces that shape their identities. The hero here is everyman, an everywoman in the guise of Italian immigrants to the U.S., who along with their children and grandchildren, are like the heroes of epics past, experience adventures and through it all achieve an awareness of the human condition worthy of passing on to new generations.

Viscusi calls this "an epic in two epochs": one being print and the other only accessible through the Internet. Thus, there is the traditional stable printed version that can be read and interpreted over time; then there's an ever-changing version that is produced by a random sonnet generator. The results are poems that resist traditional exegesis by constantly changing.

The Internet generated version creates something that can't be read the same way, making each line into what Viscusi calls "a migrant." This is accomplished by shaping each line of each sonnet into a sentence, without capitalization or punctuation, which can stand-alone, so when it is combined with any other line, it creates new meanings that seem never ending. The random sonnet generation, viewed at www.ellisislandpoem.com, is capable of more than duodecillion sonnets, the number on the book's cover.

With the wit of Martial, the rhetorical strength of Cicero, and the poetic dexterity of few others, Viscusi has created one epic poem consisting of fifty-two books made of twelve sonnets for a total of six hundred and twenty-four sonnets. The sonnets are in the fashion of Dante: fourteen lines composed into four three-line verses and a concluding couplet. And if you know technical terms like "chiasmus," you'll be able to more easily see the connection between Viscusi and the ancients, but even if the *Ars Rhetorica* is not in your range, you'll find much to ponder.

Fundamentally this is an American epic that explores the Italian coming to the U.S., the Italian American returning home to Italy, the creation of Italian America and so much more. As I read the work, I kept wondering what would happen if my grandparents listened while I read this out loud; with their ghosts over my shoulder I heard them whisper wisecracks behind his back while applauding the ways he gathers their experiences to make them matter. Maybe the ghosts won't get it, but they are it, and this explains why epics, while written of the past, belong to the future.

In his magical verses, the author captures levels of experience ranging from the personal to the public, the historical to the fantastical, reminding us that most people live epic lives that can only be recognized in art. It is the artist that sees the varieties of levels life offers to those who keep pushing to see how many lives they can pack into moments, literal and literary. In the end, *Ellis Island, the Epic*, teaches us that the antidote to reality is the poem, the antibiotic to the virus of history, and that makes Robert Viscusi the Mazzini of an Italian American Risorgimento.

Buried Caesars: and Other Secrets of Italian American Writing (Albany, NY: State University of New York Press)
ISBN: 10: 0-7914-6633-7
July 2006

Well known for his innovative insights into Italian American culture and his leadership of the Italian American Writers' Association, Robert Viscusi, a Brooklundian Professor of English and executive officer of the Ethyle R. Wolfe Institute for the Humanities at Brooklyn College, has published a long-awaited study of Italian American literature. This critic, poet, and author of the American Book Award winning novel, *Astoria*, has created an important study based on new and previously published essays that have become required reading in the field.

Buried Caesars and Other Secrets of Italian American Writing takes literary studies out of the classroom and roots them in a fine examination of "the institutional and economic base" that emerges out of the interactions of Italian and American cultures. "The abrupt way of becoming American," he writes, "left Italian Americans with a large set of beliefs that they shared and continued to pass on to their children, beliefs that had no easy entry into the general American language conversation." Viscusi calls these beliefs "Buried Caesars" because they are oppositions that "rise out of a deadly stalemate," and represent the impossibility of repressing those aspects of culture that have deeply shaped Italian American identities and affect the way we behave. Some of these "Caesars" include patriarchy, Marianist Catholicism, and mafia mania. These, Viscusi suggests, are part of "A large, slightly obscure body of beliefs that exists that Italian Americans share and that their writers confront when they sit down to explain the world".

In Viscusi's hands criticism becomes more like literary archaeology as he uncovers new layers of Italian American civilizations in the form of these "Buried Caesars," things most others have never seen. Well-versed in the classics of Italian, English, and American literatures and cultures, Viscusi has proven to be one the key theorists and developers of Italian American literary studies, producing essential reading for anyone interested in Italian American culture and the way language shapes perceptions. In some of the clearest writing he's ever produced Viscusi presents a view of literary Italian America that helps us understand aspects of the literature that only he could imagine. And like any good archaeologist, when he finds something previously unknown, he names it, as in the case of "heteroglossolalia": the act of a word from one language entering another "in the form of nonsense".

Viscusi's new essays are well connected to the old. Six of the ten have previously appeared and these have been must reading for anyone studying Italian American literature; these include his classics "De Vulgari Eloquentia," and "A Literature Considering Itself." His newer essays, "English as a Dialect of Italian," which opens the volume, "The Italian American Sign" and "The Imperial Sopranos" prove that this is a mind in its prime. The final essay in the volume, on "The Sopranos" is about the best essay you'll find anywhere exploring the origins and growth of the mafia myth in America.

This is no simple collection of previous publications. The author has fashioned an amazingly seamless narrative out of materials that have been written over a twenty-five year period. Ideas flow and follow each other as though they were composed over a shorter time span. You can tell he's revisited earlier works and in many cases revised them so that they echo earlier and anticipate subsequent chapters. If to know history is to understand the present and better imagine the future, then Viscusi has made it possible for us to do the same, and so help us to see that there is a strong future in Italian American culture. Bravo maestro!

Rolando Vitale
The Real Rockys: A History of the Golden Age of Italian Americans in Boxing 1900-1915 (RV publishing)
ISBN: 978-0-9929822-0-1
December 2015

Even if you don't care for sports, Rolando Vitale's *The Real Rockys* will give you something to talk about. *This History of the Golden Age of Italian Americans in Boxing 1900-1915* has as much to say about the Italian American experience as it does about the sport that catapulted so many young Italian American boys out of old neighborhoods and into mainstream USA.

Selected by the Order Sons of Italy for its quarterly book club, this combination history and cultural analysis contains everything you'd ever want to know about the subject, and the affect that participation in local and national sports had in the acculturation and assimilation processes. Serving equally boxing aficionados as well as anyone researching Italian American culture, *The Real Rockys* tells the story of how working class values enabled success in a time of limited possibilities.

Vitale, once a sports writer for a weekly London newspaper, has put many years into this book. His interviews, fact gathering and statistical compilations make the over 200 page Appendices worth the price alone. It's here you'll find the basis for his earlier narrative that weaves the story of hundreds of boxers through the greater Italian American history.

While many of know the more famous boxers, like Primo Carnera, Rocky Marciano and Rocky Graziano, and a few others, not many of us know that, "Many of the greatest moments in boxing in the first half of the twentieth century were . . . attributed to men of Italian lineage. Italian Americans not only captured more world boxing titles, but the sustained longevity of their success occurred in the most competitive era…" And the reason we don't know this is that these boxers' successes were often concealed behind names they took on like Hugo Kelly, "Fireman" Jim Flynn, Lou Bogash, or Johnny Dundee.

With the knowledge of seasoned scholar, Vitale writes with the clarity of a good journalist, making each chapter worthy of publication in places like *Sports Illustrated*. The first chapter covers the role boxing played in Italy. From the Greek colonization of southern Italy to gladiatorial combat in ancient Rome, through medieval and Renaissance times, and up to the nineteenth century's great migrations, Vitale's history is well researched and adds enough to previous studies to make it must reading.

Chapter 2 takes a look at the role prizefighting played in the economic development of the Italian immigrant family. Chapter 3 delves into the name changing that took place, explaining why so many young men shed their Latinate monikers and took on surnames of Irish and Jewish boxers who populated the early times of American boxing. Vitale argues that although many changed their names, most did not lose their Italian values in the process.

Chapter 4 is devoted to Casper Leon, the Sicilian born fighter who became the first Italian American fighter to gain fame and led the way to dispel predominant myths promoted by "advocates of Nativist ideology and Teutonic superiority." Many were the Italian American title claimants and contenders of this early age of American boxing. Subsequent chapters deal with "Ascendancy and inter-ethnic rivalry," the roles played by organized religion and social services, and looks at the "nature vs. nurture" argument in an attempt to explain Italian dominance in the sport. Vitale concludes by comparing boxing against baseball and football and a salient conclusion that opens the pathway for future research. The result is a valuable treasure of information that's worth its weight on your bookshelf.

Robert Zweig
Return to Naples (New York: St. Martins Press)
ISBN: 978-1-56980-351-6
May 2010

Robert Zweig is an Italian American Jew whose memoir, *Return to Naples: My Italian Bar Mitzvah and other Discoveries*, was the basis for the talk he gave at the Calandra Institute's "Land of Our Return" conference last spring, which had many people laughing. Born to a German-Jewish father and Italian mother, spent most of his childhood summers in Naples, where his mother was born and where his father came after he was liberated from a Nazi concentration camp. The memoir recounts Zweig's experiences in Naples from the time he was a young boy to today. He writes, "Nothing in Naples is bad, even for children, as long as it is diluted enough," which pertains to life experiences as well as wine, and for Zweig, the Naples he recalls today is distilled through memories.

The stories covering people and places are well written and tenderly recalled through wit and humor. The opening story, "Walking with Nonno," is a wonderful entre into the world of 1960s Italy, a time when the country is rapidly rebuilding itself into a world power. We see a growing Italy through the eyes of a growing boy. Zweig's Naples is that strange intersection of the old and new, past and present. The walk is filled with street characters including cashiers, the Bombola man, a brothel madame, a professor turned beggar, relatives and neighbors. Other characters, like Pasquale the porter to his grandparent's building, figure prominently in this coming-of-age in Italy story.

In "Revelation in Ischia" the boy learns that his father is a Holocaust survivor who lost most of his family in a concentration camp. "I Never Knew Gabriella Fabretti" presents what he learned about his mother and the reason he returned to Italy every summer. In Naples, he is the Americano, and like an ambassador, he is the lightning rod for complaints about the U.S. and the translator for national events like Kennedy's assassination and the lunar landing. "All summer I lived in a purgatorial world, immersed in Naples yet with one eye on the life I had left in New York."

A very funny segment comes in "Peeling Grapes and Other Mealtime Rituals" which, among other accounts, explains how times before one is allowed to go into the water after eating or drinking depended on what you ate: "Chocolate required eight-minutes, peaches eleven minutes, nectarines, ten, grapes one minute per four . . ."

There's humor in the little things that loom large as when an Italian printer adds the image of Jesus to Bar Mitzvah invitations thinking he is doing something extra for the Jewish boy's special day. "Where is Virgil's Tomb?" reveals that Naples is so filled with historical sites that very few residents actually know precise locations.

One of the great lessons he learns throughout the experience is how people can survive just about anything, as in this segment from "Bar Mitzvah": "Once back in the Bronx, I knew I would have more explaining to do about what kind of a Jew I was. This would be my last trip to Italy by sea, and my last long summer visit. Sensing this, I ran to the back of the ship to see the landscape slowly fading, and I listened to the muffled sounds from the port, the city's lings, expanding and contracting, until Naples too its last breath. That summer, leaving Naples, I had become a different person, having learned of a past that changed my concept of who I really was."

Return to Naples may make you laugh more than most memoirs, but it will also have you thinking about more than this young boy's life.

VIA Folios

A refereed book series dedicated to the culture of Italians and Italian Americans.

JOSEPH A. AMATO. *Diagnostics, Poetics of Time.* Vol 122. Literature. $12
DENNIS BARONE. *Second Thoughts.* Vol 121. Poetry. $10
OLIVIA K. CERRONE. *The Hunger Saint.* Vol 120. Novella. $12
GARIBLADI M. LAPOLLA. *Miss Rollins in Love.* Vol 119. Novel. $24
JOSEPH TUSIANI. *A Clarion Call.* Vol 118. Poetry. $16
JOSEPH A. AMATO. *My Three Sicilies.* Vol 117. Poetry & Prose. $17
MARGHERITA COSTA. *Voice of a Virtuosa and Coutesan.* Vol 116. Poetry. $24
NICOLE SANTALUCIA. *Because I Did Not Die.* Vol 115. Poetry. $12
MARK CIABATTARI. *Preludes to History.* Vol 114. Poetry. $12
HELEN BAROLINI. *Visits.* Vol 113. Novel. $22
ERNESTO LIVORNI. *The Fathers' America.* Vol 112. Poetry. $14
MARIO B. MIGNONE. *The Story of My People.* Vol 111. Non-fiction. $17
GEORGE GUIDA. *The Sleeping Gulf.* Vol 110. Poetry. $14
JOEY NICOLETTI. *Reverse Graffiti.* Vol 109. Poetry. $14
GIOSE RIMANELLI. *Il mestiere del furbo.* Vol 108. Criticism. $20
LEWIS TURCO. *The Hero Enkido.* Vol 107. Poetry. $14
AL TACCONELLI. *Perhaps Fly.* Vol 106. Poetry. $14
RACHEL GUIDO DEVRIES. *A Woman Unknown in Her Bones.* Vol 105. Poetry. $11
BERNARD BRUNO. *A Tear and a Tear in My Heart.* Vol 104. Non-fiction. $20
FELIX STEFANILE. *Songs of the Sparrow.* Vol 103. Poetry. $30
FRANK POLIZZI. *A New Life with Bianca.* Vol 102. Poetry. $10
GIL FAGIANI. *Stone Walls.* Vol 101. Poetry. $14
LOUISE DESALVO. *Casting Off.* Vol 100. Fiction. $22
MARY JO BONA. *I Stop Waiting for You.* Vol 99. Poetry. $12
RACHEL GUIDO DEVRIES. *Stati zitt, Josie.* Vol 98. Children's Literature. $8
GRACE CAVALIERI. *The Mandate of Heaven.* Vol 97. Poetry. $14
MARISA FRASCA. *Via incanto.* Vol 96. Poetry. $12
DOUGLAS GLADSTONE. *Carving a Niche for Himself.* Vol 95. History. $12
MARIA TERRONE. *Eye to Eye.* Vol 94. Poetry. $14
CONSTANCE SANCETTA. *Here in Cerchio.* Vol 93. Local History. $15
MARIA MAZZIOTTI GILLAN. *Ancestors' Song.* Vol 92. Poetry. $14
MICHAEL PARENTI. *Waiting for Yesterday: Pages from a Street Kid's Life.* Vol 90. Memoir. $15
ANNIE LANZILOTTO. *Schistsong.* Vol 89. Poetry. $15
EMANUEL DI PASQUALE. *Love Lines.* Vol 88. Poetry. $10
CAROSONE & LOGIUDICE. *Our Naked Lives.* Vol 87. Essays. $15

JAMES PERICONI. *Strangers in a Strange Land: A Survey of Italian-Language American Books*. Vol 86. Book History. $24
DANIELA GIOSEFFI. *Escaping La Vita Della Cucina*. Vol 85. Essays. $22
MARIA FAMÀ. *Mystics in the Family*. Vol 84. Poetry. $10
ROSSANA DEL ZIO. *From Bread and Tomatoes to Zuppa di Pesce "Ciambotto"*. Vol. 83. $15
LORENZO DELBOCA. *Polentoni*. Vol 82. Italian Studies. $15
SAMUEL GHELLI. *A Reference Grammar*. Vol 81. Italian Language. $36
ROSS TALARICO. *Sled Run*. Vol 80. Fiction. $15
FRED MISURELLA. *Only Sons*. Vol 79. Fiction. $14
FRANK LENTRICCHIA. *The Portable Lentricchia*. Vol 78. Fiction. $16
RICHARD VETERE. *The Other Colors in a Snow Storm*. Vol 77. Poetry. $10
GARIBALDI LAPOLLA. *Fire in the Flesh*. Vol 76 Fiction & Criticism. $25
GEORGE GUIDA. *The Pope Stories*. Vol 75 Prose. $15
ROBERT VISCUSI. *Ellis Island*. Vol 74. Poetry. $28
ELENA GIANINI BELOTTI. *The Bitter Taste of Strangers Bread*. Vol 73. Fiction. $24
PINO APRILE. *Terroni*. Vol 72. Italian Studies. $20
EMANUEL DI PASQUALE. *Harvest*. Vol 71. Poetry. $10
ROBERT ZWEIG. *Return to Naples*. Vol 70. Memoir. $16
AIROS & CAPPELLI. *Guido*. Vol 69. Italian/American Studies. $12
FRED GARDAPHÉ. *Moustache Pete is Dead! Long Live Moustache Pete!*. Vol 67. Literature/Oral History. $12
PAOLO RUFFILLI. *Dark Room/Camera oscura*. Vol 66. Poetry. $11
HELEN BAROLINI. *Crossing the Alps*. Vol 65. Fiction. $14
COSMO FERRARA. *Profiles of Italian Americans*. Vol 64. Italian Americana. $16
GIL FAGIANI. *Chianti in Connecticut*. Vol 63. Poetry. $10
BASSETTI & D'ACQUINO. *Italic Lessons*. Vol 62. Italian/American Studies. $10
CAVALIERI & PASCARELLI, Eds. *The Poet's Cookbook*. Vol 61. Poetry/Recipes. $12
EMANUEL DI PASQUALE. *Siciliana*. Vol 60. Poetry. $8
NATALIA COSTA, Ed. *Bufalini*. Vol 59. Poetry. $18.
RICHARD VETERE. *Baroque*. Vol 58. Fiction. $18.
LEWIS TURCO. *La Famiglia/The Family*. Vol 57. Memoir. $15
NICK JAMES MILETI. *The Unscrupulous*. Vol 56. Humanities. $20
BASSETTI. ACCOLLA. D'AQUINO. *Italici: An Encounter with Piero Bassetti*. Vol 55. Italian Studies. $8
GIOSE RIMANELLI. *The Three-legged One*. Vol 54. Fiction. $15
CHARLES KLOPP. *Bele Antiche Stòrie*. Vol 53. Criticism. $25
JOSEPH RICAPITO. *Second Wave*. Vol 52. Poetry. $12
GARY MORMINO. *Italians in Florida*. Vol 51. History. $15
GIANFRANCO ANGELUCCI. *Federico F*. Vol 50. Fiction. $15
ANTHONY VALERIO. *The Little Sailor*. Vol 49. Memoir. $9
ROSS TALARICO. *The Reptilian Interludes*. Vol 48. Poetry. $15

RACHEL GUIDO DE VRIES. *Teeny Tiny Tino's Fishing Story*. Vol 47. Children's Literature. $6
EMANUEL DI PASQUALE. *Writing Anew*. Vol 46. Poetry. $15
MARIA FAMÀ. *Looking For Cover*. Vol 45. Poetry. $12
ANTHONY VALERIO. *Toni Cade Bambara's One Sicilian Night*. Vol 44. Poetry. $10
EMANUEL CARNEVALI. *Furnished Rooms*. Vol 43. Poetry. $14
BRENT ADKINS. et al., Ed. *Shifting Borders. Negotiating Places*. Vol 42. Conference. $18
GEORGE GUIDA. *Low Italian*. Vol 41. Poetry. $11
GARDAPHÈ, GIORDANO, TAMBURRI. *Introducing Italian Americana*. Vol 40. Italian/American Studies. $10
DANIELA GIOSEFFI. *Blood Autumn/Autunno di sangue*. Vol 39. Poetry. $15/$25
FRED MISURELLA. *Lies to Live By*. Vol 38. Stories. $15
STEVEN BELLUSCIO. *Constructing a Bibliography*. Vol 37. Italian Americana. $15
ANTHONY JULIAN TAMBURRI, Ed. *Italian Cultural Studies 2002*. Vol 36. Essays. $18
BEA TUSIANI. *con amore*. Vol 35. Memoir. $19
FLAVIA BRIZIO-SKOV, Ed. *Reconstructing Societies in the Aftermath of War*. Vol 34. History. $30
TAMBURRI. et al., Eds. *Italian Cultural Studies 2001*. Vol 33. Essays. $18
ELIZABETH G. MESSINA, Ed. *In Our Own Voices*. Vol 32. Italian/American Studies. $25
STANISLAO G. PUGLIESE. *Desperate Inscriptions*. Vol 31. History. $12
HOSTERT & TAMBURRI, Eds. *Screening Ethnicity*. Vol 30. Italian/American Culture. $25
G. PARATI & B. LAWTON, Eds. *Italian Cultural Studies*. Vol 29. Essays. $18
HELEN BAROLINI. *More Italian Hours*. Vol 28. Fiction. $16
FRANCO NASI, Ed. *Intorno alla Via Emilia*. Vol 27. Culture. $16
ARTHUR L. CLEMENTS. *The Book of Madness & Love*. Vol 26. Poetry. $10
JOHN CASEY, et al. *Imagining Humanity*. Vol 25. Interdisciplinary Studies. $18
ROBERT LIMA. *Sardinia/Sardegna*. Vol 24. Poetry. $10
DANIELA GIOSEFFI. *Going On*. Vol 23. Poetry. $10
ROSS TALARICO. *The Journey Home*. Vol 22. Poetry. $12
EMANUEL DI PASQUALE. *The Silver Lake Love Poems*. Vol 21. Poetry. $7
JOSEPH TUSIANI. *Ethnicity*. Vol 20. Poetry. $12
JENNIFER LAGIER. *Second Class Citizen*. Vol 19. Poetry. $8
FELIX STEFANILE. *The Country of Absence*. Vol 18. Poetry. $9
PHILIP CANNISTRARO. *Blackshirts*. Vol 17. History. $12
LUIGI RUSTICHELLI, Ed. *Seminario sul racconto*. Vol 16. Narrative. $10
LEWIS TURCO. *Shaking the Family Tree*. Vol 15. Memoirs. $9
LUIGI RUSTICHELLI, Ed. *Seminario sulla drammaturgia*. Vol 14. Theater/Essays. $10

FRED GARDAPHÈ. *Moustache Pete is Dead! Long Live Moustache Pete!*. Vol 13. Oral Literature. $10

JONE GAILLARD CORSI. *Il libretto d'autore. 1860–1930*. Vol 12. Criticism. $17

HELEN BAROLINI. *Chiaroscuro: Essays of Identity*. Vol 11. Essays. $15

PICARAZZI & FEINSTEIN, Eds. *An African Harlequin in Milan*. Vol 10. Theater/Essays. $15

JOSEPH RICAPITO. *Florentine Streets & Other Poems*. Vol 9. Poetry. $9

FRED MISURELLA. *Short Time*. Vol 8. Novella. $7

NED CONDINI. *Quartettsatz*. Vol 7. Poetry. $7

ANTHONY JULIAN TAMBURRI, Ed. *Fuori: Essays by Italian/American Lesbiansand Gays*. Vol 6. Essays. $10

ANTONIO GRAMSCI. P. Verdicchio. Trans. & Intro. *The Southern Question*. Vol 5.Social Criticism. $5

DANIELA GIOSEFFI. *Word Wounds & Water Flowers*. Vol 4. Poetry. $8

WILEY FEINSTEIN. *Humility's Deceit: Calvino Reading Ariosto Reading Calvino*. Vol 3. Criticism. $10

PAOLO A. GIORDANO, Ed. *Joseph Tusiani: Poet. Translator. Humanist*. Vol 2. Criticism. $25

ROBERT VISCUSI. *Oration Upon the Most Recent Death of Christopher Columbus*. Vol 1. Poetry.